SHOT
AT A
BROTHEL

HAMILCAR NOIR | TRUE CRIME LIBRARY #6

PATRICK CONNOR

SHOT at a BROTHEL

THE SPECTACULAR DEMISE OF OSCAR "RINGO" BONAVENA

HAMILCAR NOIR

HARD-HITTING TRUE CRIME

ISBN: 978-1949590-27-2

Publisher's Cataloging-in-Publication Data
Names: Connor, Patrick, 1982–, author.
Title: Shot at a brothel : the spectacular demise of Oscar "Ringo" Bonavena / Patrick Connor.
Series: Hamilcar Noir
Description: Includes bibliographical references. | Boston, MA: Hamilcar Publications, 2021.
Identifiers: LCCN: 2021940544 | ISBN: 9781949590272
Subjects: LCSH Bonavena, Ringo, 1942–1976. | Boxers (Sports)—Argentina—Biography. | Boxing—History—20th century. | BISAC SPORTS & RECREATION / Boxing | BIOGRAPHY & AUTOBIOGRAPHY / Sports | TRUE CRIME / Murder / General
Classification: LCC GV1121 .B56 C66 2021 | DDC 796.83092—dc23

Hamilcar Publications
An imprint of Hannibal Boxing Media
Ten Post Office Square, 8th Floor South
Boston, MA 02109
www.hamilcarpubs.com

On the cover: Oscar Bonavena pauses before entering the ring for his fight against Jimmy Ellis at Freedom Hall in Louisville, Kentucky, on December 2, 1967.

Frontispiece: Oscar Bonavena and Dora Bonavena attend "The Fight of the Century," Ali–Frazier I, at Madison Square Garden on March 8, 1971.

To Ilian, Olivia, and Andie

OTHER BOOKS IN THE HAMILCAR NOIR
TRUE CRIME LIBRARY

Narciso
Creciente

Ablack arrow on the lower left of a photo marked what a Reno newspaper said was Oscar Bonavena.

But there was no clowning oaf or signature mop of hair. A magnifying glass may have been able to spot what the arrow pointed to: a light-colored bedsheet draped over an amorphous mound next to a new Mercury Cougar, which remained parked at a brothel's entrance.

Bonavena was under that sheet. He lay on his back, arms outstretched, head closest to the camera. Several telephone poles in the foreground failed to obscure the brothel the burly Argentine had allegedly tried to enter before he was killed with a single bullet.

Everyone in Reno knew about Mustang Bridge Ranch. In fact, a lot of people *outside* of Reno knew about this cluster of single-wide trailers and bungalows linked together. Local papers called it a "pleasure fortress."

Between the brothel and a slope of sagebrush stood a guard tower, similar to the kind found at prisons. If not for that tower the scene could have been featured in a fluff piece about a resort-style getaway in the hills. It wasn't a fluff piece; "Boxer Bonavena Slain at Mustang" read the headline in bold letters. Below the photo it said, "Mustang Ranch Brothel

Murder Scene." This was a first-draft obituary. The unsettling image—that guard tower in particular—matched the chaos that produced it, even if only abstractly.

Deep insight isn't necessary to understand the rough path that led Bonavena to Reno and into the contractual grip of local sex kingpin Joe Conforte, whose able goons guarded his beloved Mustang Ranch. Boxing has always been filled with unsavory characters; it's a world fighters are comfortable operating in. "It's the flame," Bonavena told Reno reporters while tapping hard at his chest three months before his death. "When the flame is OK, the fighter is all right." He trailed off, "When it's gone. . . ."

Bonavena's cadaver likely wouldn't have been the first one most of Conforte's crew had ever seen. A few were former law enforcement, most low-level hoods with rap sheets.

Shortly after Conforte got serious in the sex business in the mid-1950s, a turf war roiled the surrounding area along the Truckee River. Gunshots rang out, trailers were set ablaze, the old Mustang Bridge got nearly blown up. Bonavena's death was just the most famous catastrophe.

In fairness, prostitution isn't charity work and Mustang wasn't a charity. The only reason to visit Mustang was for sex, violence, or both. Sex meant money, which always needs protection.

And Bonavena loved money. More specifically, he loved money that wasn't his. Where the average person has a limit to what they feel comfortable asking of another, Bonavena had no such mechanism. He had no trouble asking for much more than most fighters would, if not demanding it, and the bridges he burned over money during his career were legion.

All of this was in addition to boxing's shameless track record of grinding up fighters and leaving them damaged and headed to an early end. Early 1900s middleweight star Stanley Ketchel and 1920s light heavyweight sensation Battling Siki were both gunned down in their twenties. Star or not, no one was immune.

The front-page story about Bonavena's death in the *other* Reno newspaper was more muted, and featured instead a different photo of the scene by the same photographer. In this one, detectives and sheriff's deputies stood in the brothel parking lot, apparently in the middle of solving the brutal crime. Just above that on the front page was a row of photos that looked like a lineup of the story's key players: Joe Conforte, his wife Sally, and the shooter, Ross Brymer.

For years Argentinian tabloids drove home the names and faces of those involved with endless coverage. They mourned Bonavena, fixated on the grand tragedy of it all, and ignored the possibility that "Ringo" had walked into this fate. But, back in Reno, each day brought another seedy detail in the news about Bonavena becoming immersed in this world of prostitution, arson, and corruption.

"He is headed nowhere because there's nowhere for him to go," said Gene Ward in the New York *Daily News* just months into Bonavena's professional career. The remark, meant to put Bonavena's shot at succeeding as a heavyweight into perspective, unwittingly augured more.

Once reality set in that Bonavena couldn't escape the grave and the official investigation progressed, the only thing clear about his slaying was the situation's murkiness; layers weren't removed but added, every detail obscuring the truth. Maybe Bonavena knew more all along than he let on, however.

"I'm going to stay in Reno," Bonavena said in one of his final interviews. "Maybe I never leave."

There are three times as many Bonavenas in Argentina as there are in Italy. Most Italian immigrants before the 1900s came to Argentina from the northern part of Italy, but they came in waves.

In the early 1900s, an eleven-year-old named Antonio Bonavena moved with his family from Calabria to Buenos Aires. Antonio later became a noted composer and bandoneonist not only in the tango genre that Argentines embraced, but also in several other kinds of music that he played with his orchestra in popular Buenos Aires clubs in the 1920s and 1930s. Antonio's brother Vicente would grow up, settle in the Buenos

Aires neighborhood of Boedo, and raise nine children: six boys and three girls.

Oscar Natalio Bonavena's life began on September 25, 1942. Bonavena's father Vicente operated a streetcar and his mother Dominga, an Italian Catholic, washed clothes and cleaned houses for extra money. They still couldn't manage to repair things, like the broken toilet eleven people shared. Bonavena stuck up for his father decades later, praising his work ethic and reminding an interviewer that Vicente was too busy with other things to even watch much television.

Like most Argentine children, Vicente's kids loved *fútbol*. Vicente Jr. was the leader, and assumed a fatherly role. In particular he tended to look out for his quirky little brother Oscar, who was born with flat feet and couldn't keep up with the other kids. Decades later Vicente was the one who took a final, somber flight back to Buenos Aires with his little brother's remains.

Even as the family struggled financially, Bonavena showed odd habits when it came to his food and clothes—behavior that continued until his death. "You never touched food on the plate he ate from," his older brother Vicente later said in an interview. "He would throw away the food, even if you just took a little bit. He would throw it away. He was crazy like that."

When the family relocated from Boedo to Parque Patricios, Oscar had trouble with local kids and Dominga encouraged her son to visit the Club Atlético Huracán, which had a boxing gym.

An urban legend circulated years later, however: Bonavena, along with Argentine boxing luminary Luis Galtieri, found himself escorted out of the San Lorenzo athletic club after urinating in view of bathers and their kids. The incident ended Bonavena's relationship with Galtieri and steered him toward the athletic club of San Lorenzo's rival, Parque Patricios.

Back in reality, Bonavena's family needed money. He took up several lower-level jobs—pizza delivery boy, working at a local quarry, and then a butcher shop—because he came from poverty and had to. There's a good chance a teenage Bonavena would have trained wherever and with whoever accepted him for that reason alone.

The awkward Bonavena nevertheless stood out even as a teenager. He was a heavily muscled boor who wouldn't shut his mouth, intent on turning attention toward him at every turn. That's why the public urination story didn't seem far off the mark.

Juan and Bautista Rago, two brothers loyal to Club Atlético Huracán, spotted a sixteen-year-old Bonavena at the gym and began the first earnest attempt at domesticating the youngster, training him and managing his career. They couldn't do anything about young love, though. At eighteen, Bonavena met and began romancing a sixteen-year-old named Dora Raffa. She later said she loved him until the morning he was murdered.

Bonavena's movement in the ring was still ponderous and awkward as a "seasoned" professional years later, so the 200-pound teenage wreck that the Rago brothers had on their hands must've been a nightmare. A testament to the patience and commitment of the Ragos, Bonavena captured the Latin American amateur heavyweight championship at age nineteen, earning a cover feature on Argentina's boxing magazine *KO Mundial*.

Although the nation's best-known boxing hero to that point, Luis Ángel Firpo, was a bit older at twenty-eight and a national treasure when placed on the cover of sports magazine *El Gráfico*, the comparisons would be swift and enduring. Argentina pushed for success in boxing on the world stage for decades and there was no better way to get it than for a native son to rise and claim the title of heavyweight champion, king of fighting men. Firpo, "The Wild Bull of the Pampas," came closer to seizing that throne than any of them.

Born in Junín in 1894, Firpo established the Argentine tradition of fighters not listening to a soul. After he eventually settled in the Boedo neighborhood, popular stories claim that three toughs attempted to rob Firpo as he walked home from his job at a brick factory and the six-foot-two Firpo flattened two of them before chasing off the third. Félix Bunge, the factory's owner, sponsored the twenty-three-year-old Firpo's start in boxing when he realized what his worker could do. Firpo insisted that he operate without a manager throughout his career, and in 1922 the South American heavyweight set out to fight in North America.

Months before he'd even arrived, American newspapers celebrated Firpo with columns that compared him to heavyweight champ Jack Dempsey and French light heavyweight king Georges Carpentier. Papers printed big photos of Firpo's warm smile and perfect hair. After a few months, Firpo went home with three knockout wins and stardom loomed.

Firpo wasted little time when he came back to the United States and headlined a Monday night Madison Square Garden show against Bill Brennan, who'd faced Dempsey twice, the second time for the title. Brennan had a difficult time with almost any good fighter, but he'd staggered the champion early in their 1920 fight and lived off of that single moment for quite some time. Three years later, Brennan was fodder for Firpo at the Garden.

The Brennan fight, won by Firpo with a twelfth-round KO, was one of six fights he had in the United States before he was matched against Dempsey by promoter Tex Rickard. At worst it was an intriguing fight on paper, as Firpo had stopped former champion Jess Willard and handled the tough Charley Weinert. In addition, Firpo sized up well physically to the champion.

Dempsey–Firpo was sloppy, brief, and savage. The fight lasted four shit-kicking minutes, and a century later it's still potent.

On a September evening in 1923, Argentines huddled around radios typically reserved for tangos, waltzes, political talk, and educational programs, captivated by their countryman trapped in a ring with an animal like Dempsey. It's hard to count the different knockdowns Firpo suffered in the chaos, even with the aid of slow-motion replay. But despite being manhandled by a fuming, vicious champion, those two rounds gave Firpo a lifetime of clout.

Firpo later got kicked out of the United States and went on to become a car salesman charged with fraud more than once, but no one remembers that. And if they did, they didn't care. In Argentina, he was a god. When Bonavena's name hit the United States, the media inevitably compared him to Firpo—as Firpo was the first connection they made between boxing and Argentina. But Bonavena and Firpo were different people, which should have been apparent from the start.

o o o

In 1943, before Oscar Bonavena reached his first birthday, Argentina had another of its regular military coups as a result of economic downturn brought on by the Great Depression and World War II. Through a complex series of events, a military leader named Juan Perón rose to power as a champion of Argentina's vast working class. Elections held in 1946 ended with Perón becoming the new president of Argentina, thanks to the *descamisados*, "the shirtless ones," a derogatory term used by anti-Perón groups that his lower-class followers then co-opted and wore with pride.

An avid sportsman in his youth, Perón promoted participation in sports and physical activities. As president, Perón sponsored fighters like José María Gatica and frequently appeared in public alongside successful athletes, perhaps in the hope that their power and strength might somehow transfer to him. When they lost, however, Perón discarded them. After Gatica fell to Ike Williams in under a round, for instance, Perón distanced himself from "El Mono." Gatica, who was embraced early on by Perón and therefore often vilified as a symbol of Peronism (and by proxy the uneducated lower class), was then shunned by the very president to whom he dedicated his entire athletic career.

Staying close to boxing, Perón and his wife Eva Duarte—diminutively known as "Evita"—could be seen at the occasional fight card at Luna Park even in the year leading to her death of cervical cancer in 1952. Amid political chaos and unrest, Argentina still readily enjoyed the fights.

News of Pascual Pérez's gold medal in the 1948 Olympics was likely too early for Bonavena to remember fully. But when Pérez overcame 6-to-4 odds to defeat Yoshio Shirai in Tokyo and win the flyweight title in November of 1954, thus becoming Argentina's first world champion, there's no way a twelve-year-old Bonavena could have forgotten all of Buenos Aires jamming the streets at 8 a.m., huddling around shops with radios to hear the ringside account.

Immediately after the official announcement at Korakuen Stadium, Pérez, a former vineyard worker and new champion, grabbed the ringside microphone and shouted, "I won for Perón! I won for my country! I won for Argentina!"

Months later Perón fled Argentina following a terrifying coup. He was forced to leave everything behind, even the body of Evita.

In 2008, an old Army veteran in New York just wanted to live to experience his seventieth birthday. A race against the colon cancer ravaging his old body underway, chemotherapy buried him in medical debt, though he'd initially refused the treatment because it killed his first wife, he said. He scrawled out an S.O.S. for the local classifieds: *NEED HELP: 69-year-old cancer patient needs bill money. Tried all I can. Any donations appreciated. Thank you. Send to: Lee W. Carr, 16 Forrest Drive, Port Jervis, N.Y. 12771-5219.* This written appeal for salvation wound up actually costing Carr money: the $4 per week ad rate added up over months, wiping out the $20 he managed to raise.

Long gone was that $500 he earned for busting Muhammad Ali's lip during a series of 1969 sparring sessions. The roughly $20,000 he'd gotten for his seventeen total professional fights was also spent long ago. A withered man, Carr said he peaked while boxing for the U.S. Army. Objectively his most notable accomplishment as a fighter was winning heavyweight gold in the 1963 Pan American Games by stopping Brazilian Jose Edson Jorge in São Paulo. After that he became a journeyman pro who couldn't get beyond a novice level, retiring in 1971 without defeating an opponent of note.

When Carr died in 2009, after having reached seventy years old, a New York newspaper recalled his connection to Ali, the Pan Am gold medal, his pro record, his stint in the Army—all standard information. What the paper didn't mention was how, in a bout leading to those same Pan Am Games finals in 1963, Oscar Bonavena bit Carr in a clinch and was disqualified. After biting Carr, Bonavena received a one-year suspension by the *Federación Argentina de Boxeo (FAB)*, no doubt punishment for the incident itself, but more important for embarrassing Argentina in Brazil, its sports nemesis.

Bonavena's assault on Carr inadvertently earned him an American introduction. A few newspapers briefly mentioned his amateur success in sports sections before he bit Carr, but the incident marked the first time anyone paying close attention to sports heard of Bonavena.

Going to the United States and turning professional was risky; Bonavena could wind up another Gatica or worse. But the suspension left him little choice considering his limited education and a lack of a family business to fall back on. With daughter Adriana on the way, he had to act fast.

Bonavena's quest for international stardom, however misguided and surely doomed, began at the fabled Buenos Aires venue, Luna Park. A few years earlier—around 1960, according to *Boxeo* by Carlos Irusta—Tino Porzio, head trainer at Luna Park, and legendary Argentine promoter Tito Lectoure, had cut a deal with manager Charlie Johnston, head of the New York Boxing Manager's Guild. Johnston had experience bringing fighters like Archie Moore, Kid Gavilán and Sandy Saddler—all of whom he managed—to fight at Luna Park. The deal allowed talent to funnel both ways to the benefit of all involved: American fighters provided a novel attraction for the growing crowds at Luna Park, and the popular Argentine fighters could, in theory, earn a title shot in the United States.

It was a clever arrangement, a step away from reviving the old tradition of far-flung locales hosting big fights and a way for a handful of

Argentines to make their way onto the U.S. scene. Few had the talent to survive and, boxing being as unforgiving as it is, the fighters typically wound up as cattle led to slaughter. Far more important, however, a door had been opened for other Argentine fighters—such as Eduardo "Zurdo" Lausse—to find success.

Restaurateur Jack Singer paid Bonavena's way to New York in late 1963. Later came Dora, who he'd since married, and newborn Adriana. In exchange for not having to wait out his suspension in Argentina, Oscar had to work in Singer's restaurant when not training. Someone in Bonavena's sphere must have known Madison Square Garden match-maker Teddy Brenner, because, in January of 1964, the twenty-one-year-old made his professional debut in a venue most pugs could never get into.

Newspapers reported a 43-2 amateur record for Bonavena. Alex Miteff, a handsome Buenos Aires native who fought most of his career in the United States, was Bonavena's trainer. Miteff had recently retired because of cuts, injuries, and bad luck, including a 1961 TKO loss to a young Cassius Clay. But Miteff did win gold at heavyweight at the 1955 Pan Am Games. And he didn't bite anyone.

Alex Miteff's story is one of boxing's oldest cautionary ones for immigrants looking to advance in a blood sport—a young, good-looking amateur destined for something more is brought to a big, fast city like New York and, short on English skills, he is eventually bilked out of his winnings by a shady manager.

In Miteff's case the manager was Hymie "The Mink" Wallman, the tough fink who acted as a front for Frankie Carbo, the notorious gangster who helped run the International Boxing Club of New York alongside James Norris. Norris, Carbo, and Carbo's partner Frank "Blinky" Palermo were ultimately key figures in a federal case against the IBC which aired much of boxing's dirty laundry. A federal investigation led by Senator

Estes Kefauver concluded that the IBC had bought fight results and paid officials—including judges in a few of Miteff's bouts.

"We Argentines," Miteff once told *Sports Illustrated*, "we don't mind being robbed, but we like you [to] tell us that you are robbing us." Then Miteff was robbed of the opportunity to make much of Bonavena.

By May 1964, an early 1900s bantamweight named Charley Goldman was hired to train Bonavena, a converted southpaw with clumsy feet. Apart from being a hands-on, no-nonsense trainer with his own ring experience, Goldman's cauliflower ears, bulldog face, black derby, and glasses gave him a sort of credibility that comes only from dank, musty boxing gyms. Goldman was a quintessential boxing stereotype.

Sportswriter Jack Cuddy described Goldman as "biscuit-faced, bespectacled gnome" and a "spry mite." Goldman said things like, "Never buy anything off the street, especially diamonds," and, "Don't tell 'em, show 'em." And, presciently, "Training a promising kid is like putting a quarter in one pocket and taking a dollar out of another."

Naturally, Goldman recognized Bonavena's punching power, but also his need for considerable refinement. Goldman had turned a raw, ham-handed Rocky Marciano into the only heavyweight champion to retire undefeated, however. If anyone could transform Oscar Bonavena into something dangerous in the heavyweight division, it was Goldman.

The main reason Goldman even entered the picture was because Bonavena began causing trouble at Singer's restaurant when he was asked to work his fair share. Bonavena ate Singer's $1.29 steaks and used the money he made at the restaurant to buy new clothes, support his family, and entertain himself. But when he was told to cut his hair, Bonavena wouldn't do it. Before long, it was as if Bonavena was doing the robbing.

Singer sold his contract to Dr. Marvin Goldberg, an optometrist and judge for the New York State Athletic Commission. Goldberg abandoned his post with the NYSAC to purchase the contract for $7,000—$5,000 for the contract itself and $2,000 for other debt Bonavena racked up.

Goldberg's fluency in Spanish may have been a factor in Bonavena's avoiding some of the early mistakes of Miteff and others. But Oscar never wavered or showed weakness around any of the business types who owned him. On the contrary, when they bought in, *he* owned *them*.

At least old Charley Goldman had been around and knew world champions were rare; he'd sparred or shadowboxed alongside hundreds of fighters just as a trainer, and five had become world champions: Al McCoy, Joey Archibald, Lou Ambers, Marty Servo, and Marciano. "One more champ," Goldman told everyone when he hooked up with Bonavena.

At the Garden on a Friday night in late May of 1964, Bonavena spent half a round flattening a Greek fighter, Byron Stoimenides, who Goldman also trained. The old trainer refused to work either fighter's corner that night.

Immediately after the card, Goldman ran into Bonavena out in front of the venue being swarmed by new fans. The trainer broke through the crowd and told Bonavena that he better show up to the gym on time the following Monday. While walking away, Goldman said to a nearby reporter, "I only wish Al Weill was around to manage this guy. He'd win the heavyweight championship for sure." Weill, who managed Marciano and Goldman's other champions, passed on handling the young Argentine after a brief inspection. He knew.

Another person who knew to stay away: Lee Carr. When Teddy Brenner contacted Carr with an offer to fight a rematch against Bonavena as a pro, Lee said, "The only way I'll fight that so-and-so is if he has all his teeth pulled."

Goldman's post-fight remark betrayed a lack of faith in Bonavena. But so what? He also doubted Marciano the first time he saw him work out on a muggy June day in 1948. And that was "The Brockton Blockbuster." But Rocky had the right head to be a fighter; he listened, and he worked on what he had learned.

"[Marciano]'s a little crude yet, to be sure," Goldman said a few fights into their relationship. "But what I like almost as much as his punching might is his poise. He has a fine temperament. Reminds me of Lou Ambers." That obviously wasn't Bonavena, who depended on roughhouse tactics and out-muscling opponents in many of his fights, frequently hitting low. He also used his forearms too much and shoved guys down. And he got tired after only a few rounds.

No matter. His opponents weren't that good yet and New York suited Bonavena. He liked being bankrolled by an overzealous and foolishly hopeful man like Goldberg, the patsy who got stuck paying for everything: restaurant bills, plane tickets to Buenos Aires, car rentals, and more. Clearly the idea of associating with a fighter who could become heavyweight champion was enough to keep the eye doctor blindly sponsoring the Argentine.

o o o

In only his sixth professional bout, Bonavena clubbed and overwhelmed Tom McNeeley, a New England heavyweight. Former champion Floyd Patterson knocked down McNeeley eleven times while defending his title in 1961. McNeely couldn't get past a world-ranked fighter on a good day, and his good days were gone.

Even so, Bonavena struggled through a swollen eye to beat up McNeeley before stopping him in five rounds, exhausting himself in front of 3,000 fans. That August night wasn't pretty, but it was a necessary fight in terms of career progression.

Then, Bonavena somehow became a headliner on a Madison Square Garden card against Dick Wipperman. A month earlier Wipperman suffered a bogus stoppage against James Beattie at the Garden and received a one-month suspension for attacking Beattie in a rage. The Bonavena–Wipperman matchup was easy to market as being potentially explosive, but, as a headliner at the Garden, it needed more than that.

In boxing no one was bigger than Muhammad Ali, and he was slated to fight his rematch with Sonny Liston three nights after the Wipperman bout, which overshadowed all other fight news. Still, Wipperman did his part, even if that meant acting like a cheap, awkwardly whitewashed version of Ali. While Ali yelled and caused a fuss, Wipperman quietly told press he'd have an easier time with Liston than Ali did, and how he was certainly "The Greatest." The New York *Daily News* mocked him, calling him a "Jewish Cassius Clay."

Bonavena said at a press conference, "If I feel good, I knock him out in one round. If I don't feel so good, maybe it take two or three." With Joe Louis and Rocky Marciano sitting ringside, Bonavena defeated Wipperman—but he settled for a decision win for the first time as a professional as Wipperman avoided him all night. Despite protesting the decision, Wipperman admitted years later that he "ran like a deer."

Bonavena got some rounds in and dealt with an opponent who didn't want to fight, which was something, but it wasn't an impressive performance. Dick Young quipped, "Oscar Bonavena, the muscle-bound Argentine goombah, wanted to fight, but doesn't know how. Dick Wipperman knows how, but didn't want to."

At least part of that was right. More likely, Oscar didn't necessarily want to fight but wanted the admiration, celebrity, and income that being a winner on a big stage brings. Boxing was simply his only way to get there.

As attendance at Ringo's fights increased, so did his confidence and tendency toward mischief. Goldberg didn't have the nerve to challenge his fighter, and by the time of the Wipperman bout, a syndicate of investors got involved.

Broadway press agent Eddie Jaffe and his protégé Tad Dowd set up International Talent and Training, or IT&T, at $250 a share, and soon a famous stripper, a noted cartoonist, a jockey, and others got in on the action. While the intention was to find investors to finance a young fighter's career, investors generally expect returns, and that was a problem. This new arrangement meant that Bonavena had more funds for boxing equipment and more good times.

Going back to the 1940s, Teddy Brenner played matchmaker for hundreds of fight cards in New York and Jersey. As such, Brenner could appreciate how curiosity in a foreign boxer could move tickets, and he got Bonavena another headlining slot at the Garden a month after the Wipperman fight. But this time Bonavena was fed St. Louis trial horse Billy Stephan, who had a far more accommodating style.

Stephan's manager, Angelo Dundee, went way back with Goldman, even seeing a young Marciano before most did—Goldman called Dundee over to assess his new prospect back in 1948. Since then Dundee had trained several world champions, but none more notable, of course, than Muhammad Ali.

Dundee praised Bonavena's left hook after Stephan took a beating for almost six rounds. Bonavena scored a knockdown in the third round and mauled his way to a sixth-round TKO victory, finishing his first year as a professional undefeated, with eight victories and seven knockouts. Money in hand, Bonavena headed back to Buenos Aires to celebrate and eat a few plates of his mother Dominga's ravioli.

Bonavena should've stayed home. He surely meant to stay longer, but Marvin Goldberg kept hounding him about signing for a fight to launch him into title contention. Specifically, Goldberg wanted Bonavena to fight against top-ten veteran Zora Folley on February 26. Newspaper reports first stated Bonavena had visa issues, which may have been true. Further prodding revealed, however, that Bonavena signed to face Peruvian Roberto Davila on February 20 in Buenos Aires.

Whether Goldberg and IT&T knew about this wasn't clear, but he couldn't seem to reach Bonavena whenever he phoned. When Goldberg sent letters or telegrams, Bonavena buttered him up by responding with veritable love letters, calling him his "American father," softening him long enough so he forgot he needed his fighter back in the United States to face a serious contender.

When Bonavena continued to balk in Buenos Aires, Teddy Brenner stepped in and called the fighter directly. The matchmaker raised Bonavena's purse from $5,000 to $7,000, and Bonavena complied. Without missing a beat, Ringo promptly told Goldberg to look elsewhere for his cut of the purse.

o o o

Pascual Pérez, Argentina's first world champion, successfully defended the flyweight title nine times despite being outweighed by several pounds each time. As is typically the case with small fighters, Pérez didn't fight long on the world-class level. Less than a decade into his career, he was all but finished and never defeated a significant fighter after losing the title to Pone Kingpetch, Thailand's first champion, in 1960.

In the last few years of his career, Pérez lost everything. His wife left him, hangers-on helped him spend the small fortune he'd amassed, and he even attempted suicide. Nevertheless he fought on, earning pocket change to fight bums. Finally, after suffering two straight knockout defeats, the FAB ordered Pérez to undergo a rigorous physical examination before he could be granted a license to fight. Already thirty-seven, Pérez retired instead in 1964.

José Gatica's and Alex Miteff's fiascos reeked of exploitation, but Pérez's case was that of a fighter unprepared to be a national hero. Pérez weighed in at only around 108 pounds for most of his career, and historically there's a direct connection between a fighter's weight and his popularity and purse. Pérez found that out the hard way when he failed to sell well in Argentina, forcing him to make over half of his title defenses abroad.

Maybe at heavyweight, Bonavena had a better chance at stardom; he was literally twice Pérez's size. He was twice the troublemaker too.

Lester Bromberg of *Boxing & Wrestling* recalled a typical episode during one of Bonavena's training sessions where Charley Goldman tried to show the young gun how to dip and pivot with a punch. Unlike many sideline trainers, Goldman never showed a fighter something unless he could get in the ring with them and do it himself. And there was Goldman, inchworming around the canvas, with his hands up and head down.

Bonavena giggled to his posse sitting ringside and stuck out his foot, tripping the old man, who caught himself. It was a bad mat, Bonavena said. Then he did it again, once more giggling to his crew.

"Tell him he'll get his head knocked off if he doesn't learn those things Charley has been trying to teach him," Brenner warned Marvin Goldberg after dropping by the gym one day. Goldberg responded helplessly: "What do you suppose I hired Goldman for originally? I wanted the best teacher—but who can get [Bonavena] to listen? I can't."

Oddsmakers initially favored Zora Folley to beat Bonavena based on experience, but the small odds gap closed and went Bonavena's way until fight time when things evened out. "He's a nice young fellow," Folley said to press beforehand, "but he's had only eight fights."

Looking back, Bonavena had no business tangling with someone of Folley's caliber at that point. Two of three judges gave Bonavena a single round out of ten and the other called it a shutout for Folley, who hammered Bonavena with a right hand seconds after the opening bell that almost sent him down. Folley even clipped Bonavena at the end of the fourth and held the sturdy Argentine up by the elbows, preventing him from suffering a knockdown.

The only round Bonavena appeared to win was the third, but it was based on his aggression alone and his questionable tactics didn't affect Folley. In the eighth, Bonavena got knocked to the canvas by a combination when Folley became tired of the pushing and mauling and let his hands go.

Just like that, at 8-1, Ringo was no longer undefeated. What's more, the injury he sustained to his left hand during the fight would affect him for years.

"Me no good; he good," Bonavena told the press afterward. Goldberg admitted sheepishly that he realized his miscalculation moments into the fight. For Folley, it was simply a necessary step toward the title shot he'd fought for twelve years to get. Bonavena was just a lumbering opponent standing in his way.

Bonavena always traveled back home to Buenos Aires when he could, but his first professional defeat established a pattern for how his international trips would go: He'd come to the United States, train, lose, and then retreat to Buenos Aires, where he was a far bigger deal and had money stashed away. Practically speaking, then, the loss didn't change anything; Bonavena was still a rising star in Argentina, still had a gorgeous wife and family, and still got his share of the $7,000 purse. Goldberg wasn't so lucky.

The New York State Athletic Commission withheld Goldberg's end of the purse pending an investigation into the syndicate backing Bonavena. When officials heard several New York writers bought into IT&T and that Goldberg had split up his own share, subletting the portions to several others, the elaborate arrangement raised red flags. The eye doctor was on his own against the commission. Bonavena went back to Buenos Aires.

Boxing doesn't make anyone crazy. To get into boxing, you have to already be a little crazy.
—José "Pepe" Lectoure

Bonavena's return home likely soothed him after his first professional loss, but Charley Goldman couldn't babysit his fighter on two continents. Thus, in Buenos Aires, Bonavena was monitored by the Rago brothers. "In South America the manager is a valet," one of Bonavena's later trainers would say, downplaying the Rago brothers' involvement. But as many found out, looking after Bonavena was a full-time job.

The only way for Bonavena to keep busy, stay in shape, and stay out of trouble was to get fights. And fights in Argentina felt more important at Luna Park. Estadio Luna Park, a short distance from Parque Patricios, was Argentina's Madison Square Garden. Any Argentine fighter was honored to fight at Luna Park, as Oscar was every time he went back.

José "Pepe" Lectoure and Ismael Pace became Argentine boxing mainstays when they made Luna Park a regular boxing venue in 1932. Lectoure's legend began in 1917, when he claimed the lightweight championship of Argentina's first official amateur tournament. Luis Ángel Firpo, the only heavyweight entrant, triumphed at the same tournament without having to throw a punch. And amid Firpo's extreme popularity, the *Federación Argentina de Boxeo* was created. With boxing now institutionalized, there was no going back.

Lectoure retired from the ring at twenty-five years old to become a manager and promoter. In 1929, one of his fighters, Justo Suarez, had an undefeated record marred by a no contest when driving rain brought an early end to a fight. Lectoure realized quickly that Buenos Aires needed an enclosed fight venue.

Pace, son of the businessman behind an older version of Luna Park, teamed up with Lectoure to build a new stadium at the site of the old one. Nearly a disaster, Luna Park was half-finished only a month out from its opening date. The doors opened officially in February of 1932 despite countless setbacks. A month later, the venue held its first boxing card during a celebration that declared Estadio Luna Park *"El Palacio de los Deportes"*—the "Sports Palace."

One week after the grand opening, Suarez lost to 1928 Olympic silver-medalist Victor Peralta—another Buenos Aires native, known as "El Jaguar"—at Luna Park. Peralta easily outboxed Suarez through ten rounds before knocking him out. Suarez fought only once more.

Even if it hadn't quite gone according to plan, the new Luna Park was christened, and its first week was a success. Boxing's popularity fluctuated in Argentina as it did across the world, although Luna Park remained a fixture throughout the 1930s, '40s, and '50s.

In 1950 "Pepe" Lectoure died, followed by his friend Ismael Pace in 1956. Ownership of the venue passed to their widows, but Lectoure's widow Ernestina Devecchi purchased a larger chunk of the park's ownership and began a secret relationship with Pepe's nephew, Juan Carlos "Tito" Lectoure.

In 1956, at only twenty years old, Tito started his rise through the ranks at Luna Park: first as a janitor and ticket-taker, then as a personnel manager. Then, at twenty-two, Tito became general manager of Luna Park.

Boxing entered something of a golden age at Luna Park under Tito Lectoure, however questionable his acquisition of power may have been.

Working under the guidance of Juan Manuel Morales, the park's official promoter, Tito nurtured the careers of fighters like Horacio Accavallo and Nicolino Locche, both of whom would go on to become Argentine boxing icons at Luna Park before Bonavena's time

While seeking refuge in Buenos Aires after losing to Zora Folley, Bonavena knocked out three unheralded opponents. The wins may have kept him in the ring but they did nothing to endear him to a public that remembered what he'd done to Lee Carr only two years earlier.

In Argentina's sports circles, Bonavena was still considered *la mancha negra,* or a black stain. A trendy haircut and some American prestige weren't fooling anyone. The public appreciated neither his bravado nor his clumsy style, which was clear in the near-mythical meeting between Bonavena and Gregorio "Goyo" Peralta in September of 1965. The fight probably did more to confirm Bonavena's role as a villain than anything before.

Peralta made his pro debut at Luna Park in 1958, and in 1963 he beat light heavyweight champion Willie Pastrano in a nontitle bout before he lost a rematch on cuts. The open-ended loss and his success in the United States—when paired with a popular last name in Argentine boxing—allowed Peralta to become a legend back home. And finally, as a gentleman, Peralta was seen essentially as the anti-Bonavena.

In his attempt to drum up interest for the fight, Bonavena called Peralta old and showed up to fight cards at Luna Park, where he told press Peralta didn't *really* want to fight him. And if Peralta did actually step into the ring with him, Bonavena said, he was going to kill him and take the Argentine heavyweight title.

The badgering worked. When the two were officially matched, Peralta received fan mail from all over Argentina while Bonavena got hate mail and threats. It was a clear good-versus-bad scenario. And although some found Bonavena entertaining, most fans wanted Peralta to knock him out.

Goldberg, still heavily invested in his fighter's career, accused the FAB of stalling when he couldn't reach Bonavena directly. In his absence, Charley Johnston used his ties to Luna Park brass to make managerial decisions. The Ragos also did their part to handle Ringo when needed.

More than 25,000 fans set an attendance and gate record in Argentina, eagerly paying to see if Bonavena could do what he promised and take Peralta out. Several thousand gathered outside Luna Park, annoyed by the lack of available tickets, and streets around the venue were choked with activity. Inside Luna Park, Bonavena arrived early and continued his antics. "Peralta, you're fighting El Cuco tonight!" Bonavena said to the press. "Say goodbye, because I'm tearing off your head!"

Bonavena may have secretly respected Goyo Peralta or found himself caught up in the moment, but the fight was slower than anticipated because of Bonavena. It wasn't until round four that Bonavena opened up and started mauling, forcing Peralta to hold, which made the action even messier. Both fighters drew warnings, but the crowd was getting into it, surging with the energy that sweeps through fight crowds.

Then, with a single left to the chin, Bonavena silenced the crowd of 25,000, even if briefly. Everyone watched in shock as Peralta dropped to his knees. After somehow rising and surviving, Peralta made a final stand in the ninth round, matching Bonavena punch for punch in spots and bringing fans to their feet. It was close and Peralta may have won the round, but he gave up almost twenty pounds to Bonavena plus a lot of strength. In the end, Peralta's effort and the crowd's zeal weren't enough, and Ringo won a comfortable twelve-round decision.

In a later interview with *El Gráfico*, Bonavena said, "Peralta said he was going to trash-talk back [to me], then later on he was quiet. After the fight, I invited him to come to my house and eat my mom's ravioli and he didn't show up. What a weirdo."

If this confused him, it showed that Bonavena didn't understand that everyone was not like him. Not all fighters can sling insults, engage in nasty trash talk, and then turn it off when a fight ends. That requires either promotional genius or something else. And Bonavena was no promotional genius.

○ ○ ○

As Bonavena celebrated his defeat of Peralta, Joe Conforte sat in a federal prison 7,000 miles away at McNeil Island, Washington, nearing the end of a three-year bid for tax evasion. Three weeks earlier, in mid-August 1965, a few trailers owned by Conforte burned to the ground in an unexplained fire. He'd been moved from Terminal Island in California to McNeil Island for, he said, "causing too much trouble."

"A guy like me goes to prison and you have it about as good as you can get," Conforte said later. He ran prison scams and paid other prisoners to work for him inside. He claimed his cellmates at McNeil Island included disgraced Teamster president Dave Beck, notorious gangster Alvin "Creepy" Carpis, and Frankie Carbo, a Lucchese crime family *soldato* (soldier) whose shady dealings in boxing led *Sports Illustrated* to once call him "the underworld commissioner of boxing."

Conforte knew a few boxing figures before his big prison stint. In fact, a 1959 arrest alongside a former fighter named Jimmy "Kid" Williams initiated the series of events that sent Conforte to prison. And Williams spent eighteen months at McNeil Island himself.

But Carbo was on another level. He spent four years at a juvenile reformatory at age eleven and committed his first known murder at twenty. Over the next fifteen years he was charged with murder five times and arrested many more, serving a sentence in the infamous New York prison Sing Sing. He'd picked up several nicknames such as "Jimmy the Wop," "Mr. Fury," "The Ambassador," and the best-known, "Mr. Gray."

In the mid-1930s, Carbo began buying percentages of managerial contracts of fighters, starting with middleweight champions Al Hostak, Babe Risko, and Solly Kreiger. His boxing involvement eventually guided him to Mike Jacobs, New York promoter and head of the Twentieth Century Sporting Club, the fight world's premier promotional outfit. Jacobs promoted heavyweight champion Joe Louis, who reigned from 1937 to 1949, exerting his influence over boxing through its biggest and most powerful player.

Jacobs suffered a stroke just after World War II ended in 1946 but retained control of his promotional company. James Norris, a sports investor and businessman, formed the International Boxing Club of New York alongside his friend Arthur Wirtz and Louis, who they paid $150,000 to retire, effectively ending the Jacobs era. At some point Norris struck up a friendship and business relationship with Carbo, and by the early 1950s they controlled dozens of fighters through an elaborate shell game of gangsters posing as managers who would muscle in on established fighters' contracts and take control of their careers.

There was at least one experienced manager, Al Weill, who became friends with Carbo and Norris. An avid horse-racing bettor, Norris owned several horses and named one "Mr. Gray" after Carbo, and another "Al W." after Weill. During this time Weill was still developing an emerging fighter named Rocky Marciano.

The IBC was well-known as a powerful and potentially danger-ous entity in boxing, but the motivation for taking over an entire wing of the sport was money. The IBC effectively owned the coveted heavy-weight championship and guided other title fights, which allowed for control over sports betting and gave cover for other mob-related activi-ties. Carbo's managers and reputation as a killer gave him leverage even within the structure of the IBC. But he began, however, to reach too far.

In the mid-1950s it became difficult to do business in boxing on the East Coast or Midwest without going through the IBC. In 1956, the National Boxing Association called for a federal investigation into racketeering operations in boxing and Norris openly taunted that the IBC was "not afraid of any federal investigation in boxing." Immediately, intense fed-eral scrutiny followed and the government in 1958 charged Carbo with conspiracy, operating as a manager without a license, and operating as a matchmaker without a license. He was sentenced to time at Rikers Island the following year. A 1960 Senate hearing revealed the inner work-ings of the IBC, and in 1961 charges of conspiracy and extortion stemming from the IBC's handling of welterweight champion Don Jordan got Carbo a twenty-five-year sentence at McNeil Island.

The extent of Carbo and Norris's influence in boxing during the 1950s has been challenged over the decades, notably by author W. C. Heinz and lawyer/promoter Truman Gibson. But Carbo's dark history couldn't be questioned. He was a homicidal mobster deeply involved in the careers of many fighters, and wearing a nice suit and staying quiet only obscured the facts. He was powerful and not to be fucked with.

That was the kind of gangster Joe Conforte wanted to be. In reality he was a struggling brothel owner, but he still tried to play the part. As Conforte waited for his November 1965 release from prison, his wife Sally told a *Nevada State Journal* reporter she'd be waiting for Joe with a chauffeured limousine, "Even if I have to buy a cap and drive the car myself."

He could have theoretically been influenced by something Mr. Gray said at McNeil Island, but whatever the impetus, Conforte changed tactics after his release. His plans still involved brothels and sex and crime, of course, but he needed a better cover. Fortunately, he hadn't lost much of his local popularity while locked up.

"I never imagined I have so many friends," Conforte told the *Reno Gazette* after his release. "And I haven't been able to pay for a thing in any of the clubs."

○ ○ ○

The media measured Bonavena against Luis Firpo ceaselessly, and the more time went by, the clearer it became that Bonavena was no Firpo. "[Bonavena] is a much better fighter than Firpo, who depended solely on strength," Charley Goldman told sportswriter Harry Grayson. "This guy is just a good all-around fighter. He will never be called the New Bull of the Pampas." Only one of those three statements was true, and it wasn't the first two.

Firpo endeared himself to the public by beating a few solid American fighters before proving himself versus a monster. On a personal level he was a rascal, but otherwise good-natured and usually gracious. Bonavena, on the other hand, acted entitled and had failed his first significant test.

Then he compounded the public's resentment by disrespecting Peralta. Realizing this resentment could still be monetized, Tito Lectoure made sure Bonavena's visibility increased in Argentina by encouraging more local magazine interviews and public appearances. Bonavena appeared at Luna Park fight cards often, and starting in 1965, *El Gráfico*, Argentina's most popular sports magazine, featured Bonavena on its cover regularly.

Bonavena added two stay-busy wins in October 1965 before Lectoure lured American journeyman Billy Daniels to Luna Park, where he was beaten inside one round. Daniels had lost previously to Muhammad Ali, Zora Folley, Cleveland Williams, Doug Jones, and Thad Spencer—but never as fast. When asked afterward why he was in such a hurry, Bonavena said he had a singing gig with an orchestra early the next morning and he wanted to get the fight over with.

The nickname "Ringo" showed how much Bonavena relished attention. He embraced his connection to the Beatles drummer by releasing a rock single called "Pio, Pio, Pa" in late 1965. The groove attempted to mimic that early Beatles swing, but, not surprisingly, it sounded thrown together and amateurish. Yet in Argentina it still sold almost 20,000 copies in two weeks.

Bonavena took a few months off before returning with another quick knockout in February 1966 before accepting a fight in March against José Giorgetti, an Argentine Olympian who briefly held the FAB heavyweight title and weighed about 30 pounds more than Bonavena. Maybe the fame started getting to Ringo, unraveling him a bit. It's also possible he simply started believing his own hype. According to Bonavena, when he battered Giorgetti to the canvas with a legal punch, the referee, confused, took Bonavena to a neutral corner and began examining him instead. As that happened, the bell to end the eighth round rang and Giorgetti came to life before saying he could no longer continue.

News reports, however, stated that Bonavena was simply disqualified for repeated roughhouse tactics and hitting Giorgetti low. The newspapers were more believable.

A Bonavena–Giorgetti rematch headed for Luna Park a month later, and this time Bonavena kept his head and won a decision, which set up another attempt to court American audiences. In May, Teddy Brenner announced that Bonavena would fight iron-chinned Canadian slugger George Chuvalo at Madison Square Garden sometime in July. Bonavena almost turned the bout down, once more driving a harder bargain than was merited. Goldberg stepped in to make the fight happen, personally guaranteeing Bonavena $10,000 despite being heavily in debt already, and knowing it was unlikely that he'd see much from Bonavena's payday. Satisfied, Bonavena agreed to terms. He arrived in New York from Buenos Aires one month out.

While the Chuvalo fight isn't typically listed among Bonavena's most important or memorable bouts, it was certainly telling, if not an indication of things to come. Chuvalo trained at Kutsher's Country Club while Bonavena and his team stayed at Grossinger's Resort, a sprawling hotel and resort in the Catskill Mountains that was used by countless big-name fighters. Bonavena fell in love and half-jokingly requested a two-week singing gig at Grossinger's nightclub in exchange for defeating Chuvalo.

Boxing is a sport of styles. And Bonavena, often short on substance, relied largely on his style to see him through. As opposed to outfoxing his opponents in the classical boxing sense, he browbeat them into submission and worked off their bewilderment. Chuvalo knew that.

"I've heard about this guy Bonavena," Chuvalo told United Press reporters before the fight. "A friend of mine has seen a lot of fights in South America and says the guy will try anything he can get away with. If he does, I'll retaliate." Odds hovered around 9-to-5 for Chuvalo, who lost in fifteen rounds to heavyweight champion Muhammad Ali on just seventeen days' notice a few months earlier and fought twelve rounds with former champion Floyd Patterson in a highly entertaining 1965 showdown.

At the eleventh hour, Bonavena refused to leave his hotel room until he received a cash advance on the purse. As expected, a fight between two physical, blockish men who tended to lurch and crouch around meant a busy night for referee Arthur Mercante. Both boxers were warned for infractions stemming from collisions and wrestling with each other, but, to his credit, Bonavena stayed busy and attacked the body regularly. He actually looked like he fought with a plan in mind and executed it by darting in and out and even moving laterally, as awkward as it looked.

Chuvalo, stylistically a deliberate, plodding counterpuncher, looked even slower as he stood straight up in front of Bonavena, trying to match his pace and approach. In round two Chuvalo got knocked off-balance by a left hand and his glove almost touched the canvas, and in round four a combination of a misstep and a grazing Bonavena right hand sent Chuvalo into the ropes.

Those two moments, however fleeting in real time, gave rise to the legend that Bonavena actually knocked Chuvalo down. But Chuvalo never went down. After ten rounds were done, Mercante scored the fight even. Two judges who believed Bonavena deserved the win overruled him.

An Argentine flag sailed over the top rope and draped over Ringo's shoulder immediately after the decision was announced. A handful of fans even rushed into the ring to congratulate Bonavena, who had just scored by far his best victory yet. "Patterson and Clay, all in one day!" Bonavena kept repeating to reporters between belting out opera and contemporary rock hits.

By 1966, heavyweight champion Muhammad Ali was no longer Cassius Clay, despite major publications like the *New York Times*—and even *The Ring* magazine—still calling him Clay in headlines. Almost everyone did it, even if they weren't always doing it maliciously.

In 1965 the World Boxing Association refused to continue recognizing Muhammad Ali as their champion when he signed to fight a rematch against Sonny Liston, splitting the heavyweight title on paper. Even so, Ali was still very much the champion.

A few nights after Bonavena–Chuvalo, contenders Ernie Terrell and Doug Jones fought in Houston for a meaningless World Boxing Association heavyweight title. Ali watched Terrell and Jones fight for his championship from a New York movie theater and complained the fight was boring, even yawning exaggeratedly to theatergoers. As Ali talked to fans afterward, Bonavena walked down the aisle and shoved his hand into Ali's.

"Go to Europe," Bonavena told him. "Then come to South America and fight me."

Ali dismissed Bonavena outright and said something about the Argentine being crazy. Then he moved on with his life.

When the United States committed almost a half-million troops to Vietnam in 1966, it changed everything. In August, Secretary of Defense Robert McNamara announced the Defense Department's intention to call an additional 100,000 men previously ruled ineligible for military draft. Almost all of these additional troops were poor and uneducated, and most belonged to minority groups. The decision would be called "Project 100,000." Muhammad Ali fit right in.

Ali—or "Clye," as Bonavena called him through a thick accent—was already a controversial figure: some ridiculed him because they believed the Nation of Islam used him as a pawn, while others viewed him as a beacon of revolutionary hope. When Ali changed his name from Cassius Clay to Cassius X and then Muhammad Ali, even neutral publications took a political stance in how they chose to refer to the heavyweight champion. In fact, *The Ring*, boxing's most respected magazine in the United States, took eight years (and fifty-nine issues) to call Ali by his name on cover features.

The name change became a point of contention throughout Ali's career. In 1967 he famously screamed, "What's my name?" again and again while battering Ernie Terrell, who refused to call him Ali.

When Ali declared his intention to refuse being called for service, a number of boxing figures and organizations prepared for a vacant heavyweight title. Sure enough, the U.S. Army reexamined Ali at an Armed Forces induction center in Houston and declared him fit to serve in April

1967. The NYSAC and WBA stripped him of all recognition immediately. New York even revoked his license. Two victories over a monster like Sonny Liston didn't mean as much if Ali couldn't get licensed to fight.

Ali went back to his hotel room in Houston and called his mother back home in Louisville, wiping tears from his eyes as he told her what just happened, aware his boxing career may have been finished at only twenty-five years old. Asked who he thought would succeed him as champion, Ali replied, "Oh, they'll pick up some dodo or junior champion."

The WBA was a boxing governing organization previously known as the National Boxing Association. In many respects it counteracted the influence of the NYSAC and its rankings in the 1920s and 1930s, and in the 1960s it began cooperating with an alliance of international governing bodies.

Newspapers reported that Bonavena would challenge Terrell for his paper title in September of 1966. Another former Olympian whose name would forever be tied to Ali's, Joe Frazier, a left-hooking swarmer out of Philadelphia, got to Bonavena first. Immediately after Frazier defeated Billy Daniels in July, Frazier's handler Yank Durham contacted Teddy Brenner asking to fight the "Ringo of the Ring." At 11-0 following his first year as a professional, Frazier had yet to go the distance.

Bonavena retreated to Buenos Aires and this time Brenner followed him to discuss terms and get a contract signed. By early August, the fight was signed for September 21 at Madison Square Garden.

On returning to the United States, Bonavena predictably went back to Grossinger's to train while Frazier trained at the Concord Hotel Resort, also in the Catskills. Bonavena continued to burn through everyone's money except his own as he kept valuable cars, property, and businesses in Buenos Aires. Despite investing wisely in Argentina, he still badgered Marvin Goldberg and associates for cash regularly.

It wasn't enough, however. During one of his prefight workouts at Grossinger's, Oscar told reporters that he wanted to be backed by a group of businesspeople and investors, like Frazier had with Cloverlay, Inc. Instead, Oscar's syndicate was a collection of random stiffs whose investments were divided and sold off already. What's more, Bonavena even traded Charley Goldman for trainer Sid Martin, an experienced East Coast trainer found often at Stillman's Gym.

"Fighters need lots of lawyers now," Bonavena said. "Every champion in every division had a lawyer doing business for him. That seems to be the way to win a title. A couple of bankers won't hurt either."

The interview was either translated or completely spoken on his behalf. Bonavena's English just wasn't that good. But the point was clear: Bonavena believed a title could be bought, and if he couldn't find a clear path to one it meant he had the wrong people in his corner. To him a championship wasn't something that must be earned. As with show business, success in boxing involves contacts and personal favors as well as merit—so to some degree Bonavena was right. But a fighter can't rely entirely on greased palms. In the end, a fighter must still fight.

Bonavena eased himself into the business discussion, demanding Brenner also give up 100 percent of Argentine film rights to the Frazier bout. Brenner almost screwed up the entire deal when he accidentally signed the rights away to a different company and Bonavena refused to fight. Not surprisingly, the show proceeded only when the Garden came up with some extra money.

In the last few days leading to the fight, the NYSAC requested that Bonavena cut his hair, to the Argentine's dismay. "The commission gets me angry," Bonavena told an Associated Press reporter. "They want me to cut my hair. I tell them no. I am like Samson. If I cut my hair I will lose my strength."

The NYSAC didn't press the issue, and Bonavena kept his mop.

o o o

Most pundits suggested the Frazier–Bonavena meeting was simply a litmus test for Frazier, reasoning Bonavena could take a good punch, wouldn't be difficult to hit, and wasn't a big puncher himself. But Yank Durham and the press either misjudged Ringo's punching power or didn't realize Joe's constant forward momentum and leaping would recklessly lead him into something wild. Or both.

A surprising crowd of over 9,000 showed up to the Garden on an incredibly rainy Wednesday night, including enough Bonavena fans to cut through the usual din with chanting. Bonavena appeared almost rattled by Frazier's brute strength as Frazier plowed forward in the opening round. Ringo was unaccustomed to seeing a guy his size tearing at him the way Frazier did, mouthpiece exposed through a sawtooth grin.

In round two, Bonavena swung back with fervor and Frazier pursued, appearing steady in the face of Bonavena's shots. Then just over one minute into the round, Bonavena inched backward out of a clinch and stared straight through Frazier, who foolishly threw a lazy jab while looking for a right hand. Bonavena saw it and dodged the punch by pulling his upper body back, then countered with a jab and right hand that dropped Frazier onto his back.

Several well-dressed men ringside threw up their arms as if to urge Frazier off the canvas. The Olympic gold medalist rose to his feet at the count of four on unsteady legs and staggered to the ropes. When the action resumed, Bonavena cuffed Frazier with left hooks as Frazier reached out to hold on. One hook caught Frazier's ear, knocking him backward and straight down to the mat, although not as violently this time. When Frazier bounced up at the count of two, about half of the round remained.

This was Bonavena's chance. He had an unbeaten commodity teetering in front of him, ready to be knocked down a third time, which would have meant an automatic technical-knockout win. Bonavena barged in and landed a right hand before falling into Frazier's clinch. Like a novice, he stifled his punches, killing his chances by pushing forward recklessly. He should have composed himself and found the right distance, or gone to the body to bring Frazier's gloves down if he couldn't help but fight inside. But he didn't, and even worse he rocked out of a clinch with a bad cut over his left eye.

With thirty seconds remaining, Frazier found his composure and smiled his way to the bell. It was part relief, part taunting, as if to say, "You just lost your chance, pal." Still, Cloverlay, Inc. was nervous after that disastrous round.

Yank Durham later told *Sports Illustrated*, "[Frazier] wasn't moving like he should—side to side, slipping punches, ducking under, coming in and punching at the same time."

Round three unfolded almost as if the previous round never existed because Frazier began doing those exact things. Bonavena mostly retreated, about half of his offense consisting of pushing off as Frazier got him to the ropes and banged away.

Frazier softened Bonavena up with body shots and caught him with several hard hooks to the head while Bonavena continued to retreat between failed attempts at landing another blockbuster right hand. When Bonavena fell into clinches—which was often—he draped himself over Frazier, who continually freed his gloves and schooled the Argentine on the basics of fighting at close range.

Bonavena certainly tried to get right hands to land, but telegraphed punches don't typically connect. Pushed back too often and unable to plant his feet and throw a left hook with conviction, Bonavena lost several rounds and allowed Frazier to make up the points he'd lost for getting knocked down.

In the middle of round six, Frazier's output dropped and he began tiring, bringing the fight down to street level, which suited Bonavena just fine. But Frazier's right hands, which weren't even his best punches, were still more effective than Bonavena's.

Frazier continued working Bonavena's hips in the seventh, drawing a warning from the referee and visible complaints from Bonavena, whose cut bled freely the entire time. In the eighth, Bonavena backed to the ropes continually and braced for punches by doubling over, but they landed hard anyway.

Madison Square Garden's play-by-play man, the venerable Don Dunphy, spoke too kindly of Bonavena on the televised broadcast. Apart from two rounds, he had been mostly outfought and at times beaten up.

In round ten, Bonavena took a long, deep breath and dug in to exchange with Frazier, finding success once more by bouncing around and timing Frazier on his way in. The Madison Square Garden crowd appreciated a stirring, albeit sloppy, end to the bout. When the final bell rang, Frazier smiled and grabbed Bonavena around the neck as the Argentine huffed his way around the ring exhausted.

The split-decision win for Frazier was fair. In close rounds Frazier's body punching filled gaps in the action while Bonavena pushed off, looking for space and perhaps time. Frazier also set the pace as the aggressor all evening. The crowd still didn't like the result, booing it even as Dunphy interviewed Frazier for television.

NYSAC doctor Harry Kleiman told Jim McCulley of the New York *Daily News* that Bonavena suffered several contusions on his hip from being hit. Sid Martin complained loudly enough to referee Mark Conn about low blows that a commissioner at ringside ordered Martin to report to NYSAC offices for a hearing. A disappointed Bonavena and his team talked about protesting the decision and the fight's officiating before heading to the hospital. Yet again he'd been beaten in front of an American audience, which meant it was time to buoy himself in Buenos Aires.

There was something Bonavena could take home with him, though: he took Frazier the distance for the first time. Robert Lipsyte of the *New York Times* wrote from ringside, "Bonavena, who has been called a bum and an animal, never quit." Technically correct, Lipsyte might not have known Bonavena smashed his fist through a dressing room door at the Garden after the fight.

Bonavena retreated to Buenos Aires with another loss, his record now 21-3.

On October 1, 1966, shortly after Bonavena arrived home, two of his old foes, Eduardo Corletti and Jose Giorgetti, met in a Luna Park main event. At some point during the show, Bonavena entered the ring and trashed both fighters, trying to work the crowd a bit. The FAB wasn't amused and stripped him of their heavyweight championship for "unruly and unsportsmanlike attitudes."

In almost any interview around this time, Bonavena was liable to mention "Clye" as a desired opponent—and nobody could blame him for it. Ali was the champion, sanctioning organizations be damned, but he was also controversial and notorious to the degree that his opponents' lives were forever changed simply by facing him. Perhaps the stunt at the Corletti–Giorgetti bout was an attempt to steal the champion's heel act, but performed by someone incapable of reading the room.

Bonavena fought nine times between October of 1966 and August of 1967. Four of those nine bouts took place at Luna Park, including a ten-round decision win over Amos Johnson, an American who'd defeated former British heavyweight champion Henry Cooper and no one else of note. Bonavena also found time to wipe out Giorgetti in their rubber match.

The WBA wasted little time in proposing an eight-man tournament, confirming plans just hours after Ali left the Houston induction center. The NYSAC quickly agreed to cooperate, and the fighters initially billed to participate in the tournament were Joe Frazier, Ernie Terrell, Floyd Patterson, Karl Mildenberger, George Chuvalo, Jimmy Ellis, Thad Spencer, and Bonavena.

Cloverlay held a vote and decided the money the tournament promised wasn't worth tying up Frazier for roughly two years. Instead he would continue to hammer away at the division's peripheral contenders.

Jerry Quarry and Leotis Martin replaced Frazier and Chuvalo, whose team declined on his behalf, but the matches came together quickly: The winners of Ellis–Martin and Bonavena–Mildenberger would meet the winners of Quarry–Patterson and Spencer–Terrell, respectively.

As Bonavena wrapped up his nine-fight run, a company called Sports Action, Inc., teamed with television network ABC to organize the WBA's eight-man tournament. Madison Square Garden tried to lock down several of the tournament's participants for its own matchups, causing Sports Action, Inc., to throw money around and book everyone first. The Garden was familiar with this tactic and worse, as it had survived the Mike Jacobs era.

Sports Action, Inc.'s tactics sparked concerns about purse inflation, making the tournament's legitimacy easy to question since three of the eight fighters had been defeated by Ali already, and the rest had thin records. The fat purses ensured contracts got signed, and the tournament moved forward quickly regardless of media skepticism. The winner would hold a portion of the heavyweight title, which would be effectively owned by Sports Action, Inc.

Bonavena's opponent, Karl Mildenberger, was a German veteran legitimized by Ali on the champion's 1966 European tour. Mildenberger looked little more than awkward and tough in losing to Ali by a twelfth-round stoppage but the German was the European heavyweight champion and that apparently meant enough to get him into this round-robin.

This time, while Bonavena was in Buenos Aires tending to his various businesses and whatever else, Marvin Goldberg sold off even more of his shares in IT&T. The syndicate itself was broken up when NYSAC officials found that no one involved agreed on the terms of their contracts or how much money they were actually entitled to.

It was all academic. Bonavena bought two pairs of everything, from boxing gloves and shoes to expensive gym bags and clothes. Goldberg was contractually owed one-third of Bonavena's purses, but the fighter would simply claim insolvency. Skipping town after fights was merely one of his tactics to avoid paying his team. This left Bonavena in the hands of Lectoure and the Rago brothers.

Likely sensing a chance at being associated with a fighter competing at the international level, the FAB reinstated Bonavena as their heavyweight champion. He could always catch some kind of break at home, and it was that type of enabling that allowed his self-worship to grow.

A Great
Pantomime

I n early August 1967, Jimmy Ellis defeated Leotis Martin and Thad Spencer beat Ernie Terrell on a Houston fight card. Meanwhile, with a $50,000 guarantee in hand, Bonavena caught a plane to Frankfurt in September, intent on bowling over Karl Mildenberger on his own turf. Germans welcomed the fight enthusiastically. Apart from Ali–Mildenberger having taken place recently, it was the first ever heavyweight championship bout fought in Germany. Additionally, Mildenberger became the first left-handed fighter to challenge for the title. The novelty hadn't worn off.

Bonavena–Mildenberger was supposed to be a natural next step toward drawing more major fighters to Germany, and Bonavena, whose managerial and financial issues had been covered widely in print to this point, was made a 4-to-1 underdog. All Mildenberger had to do was win. But it was a fiasco from top to bottom.

First, his managers, the Ragos, were kicked out of Mildenberger's camp for reportedly trying to spy on sparring sessions. Then, during the week of the fight, promoter Joachim Goettert moved Bonavena's training quarters into the same building as Mildenberger and did so without telling the German's former manager, who owned the place. German reports then dismissed Bonavena outright when he looked thoroughly subpar in sparring against Argentine light heavyweight José Humberto Menno. Then there was the fight.

"It ranks as one of the worst conducted fights I have seen in my entire career," said founder and editor of *The Ring*, Nat Fleischer. In place of a bell, the timekeeper banged on a bean can with a padded mallet. No one could hear it. Bonavena scored knockdowns in rounds one, four, seven, and ten, and the timekeeper didn't even know to administer a count until the final one.

After the third knockdown, referee Harold Krause shouted, "God, will someone please do some counting?" Even with several knockdowns, it was a tedious night. Mildenberger slogged his way to the final bell after twelve rounds, chasing a mostly defensive Bonavena and having likely only won a single round, the ninth. Not even Bonavena's numerous low blows and kidney punches could derail his win.

Some 18,000 funereal Germans watched as the flat-footed South American hippie celebrated his advance toward a world-title opportunity as a unanimous decision went his way. Bonavena's win represented "a blow to the tournament," *Sports Illustrated*'s Mark Kram said. "To think of Bonavena in the company of [Jimmy Ellis and Thad Spencer] is an obscenity."

In response to Kram's column, titled "A Bean-Can Bout in Frankfurt," Goldberg wrote to *Sports Illustrated* three issues later disputing Kram's perception of Bonavena as a money-guzzling cartoon. Of course, Goldberg could have personally confirmed most of Kram's accusations. Instead, he defended his own delusion, likely grasping at the hope that Bonavena as heavyweight champion would justify the suffering—a gambler's mentality through and through. The doctor absorbed the debt Bonavena racked up and looked like a common mark.

Kram's article confirmed that Bonavena had already worn out his welcome in a few key boxing circles and, consequently, American media generally wasn't interested in examining him with a discerning eye. His reputation in the United States was that of a foreign boor who mimicked Tarzan yells and threw semi-playful body shots at reporters like Howard Cosell mid-interview. In many ways it was just another cheap Ali impression, but to enjoy this one you needed subtitles.

More plainly, Bonavena fought like a bully. Like most bullies, of course, he faltered when someone stood up to him. Since Mildenberger couldn't do that, he became fodder for the Argentine. One year later, the German's career was over.

Bonavena flew into Ezeiza International Airport in Buenos Aires a week after the bout. The roof of the terminal was filled with onlookers and thousands gathered at the airfield to greet him. Among them were his mother, several fighter friends, and the Argentine press. Ringo's meaty fists stuck out of the sleeves of his expensive Italian coat as he raised his arms triumphantly. A police escort then led him home.

Bonavena picked up a nagging back injury fighting with Mildenberger, which affected the tournament's schedule. As Bonavena rested, Jerry Quarry narrowly defeated former champion Floyd Patterson at the Olympic Auditorium in Los Angeles. Most newspapers , including the *Los Angeles Times*, thought "Irish" Jerry was lucky to get the win.

Growing restless, the WBA and Sports Action, Inc., threatened to replace Bonavena with Frazier when Ringo suddenly got better in time to face Jimmy Ellis in December. Ellis typically trained out of Miami Beach at Angelo and Chris Dundee's 5th Street Gym. He was a skilled heavyweight with good legs, deft movement, and an excellent jab—and he'd sparred numerous hours with Ali. Angelo also trained Ali before the champ's excommunication, and he knew a counterfeit when he saw one.

A few weeks before the fight, Bonavena arrived in Louisville and both men worked out at Bud Bruner's gym. Bruner knew boxing, having been involved in the Louisville Golden Gloves for years and organizing Olympic boxing trials in 1956 and 1960. And Bruner knew Ellis, who he trained and managed for the first twenty fights of Ellis's pro career.

Often Ellis's training would overlap with Bonavena's or they would both stick around the gym to get badgered by local newspaper writers.

One day in Bruner's gym, Bonavena began loudly ranting, calling himself the champion in Spanish. "They all try to imitate [Ali] now, don't they?" Angelo remarked, smirking. "What they don't know is that there was only one [Ali], and there'll never be another like him."

Bonavena even picked up a Santa Claus suit and walked around downtown Louisville challenging other Santas to fight him. In the gym he barked and loudly smacked the bags. He would do nearly anything to draw attention to himself, and small-town Americans just didn't understand any of it. Even if people in big cities did understand him, they were annoyed by him too.

Charley Goldman, who let Bonavena into his gym when several others declined to handle him—and was dismissed from the team from half a world away in Buenos Aires for his trouble—had recently gone through a health scare. For whatever reason, Oscar told writers he'd be dedicating the Ellis fight to Goldman. It was classless.

If Ellis had a specific problem in the ring, it was that he got stuck with what trainers refer to as "sparring-partner mentality": Ellis would stop punching when he had a fighter hurt, or he would simply cover up and allow an opponent to work him over on the ropes. It led writers to discount him, and declare that he'd never be more than Ali's former sparring mate. Even Angelo Dundee sometimes expressed doubts.

But in front of roughly 4,000 spectators at Freedom Hall in Louisville, Ellis found the identity he'd been looking for: Only four years removed from being a much smaller middleweight, Ellis delivered on his potential against a young, strong fighter who should've been able to push him around.

No one was worried about Bonavena outmaneuvering Ellis, who knew as many tricks as anyone, but Dundee specifically told the press about his concern that Bonavena would somehow corner Ellis and work him over against the ropes. As it turned out, that concern was unfounded.

Ellis missed a left hand just moments into the fight, and it seemed to convince Bonavena to fight defensively. Ellis actually gave chase because Bonavena wouldn't engage. Then, in round three, a right hand hit Bonavena on the temple and he went down. He struggled to find his legs for a few moments, and Ellis let him off the hook.

After taking a round to recover, Bonavena finally began rushing in, and Ellis's jackhammer jab slowed down, allowing the Argentine to adjust his range without issue. The problem was that Bonavena simply mauled and cuffed and rarely landed a clean punch in close.

In round eight, the rough tactics paid off when Ellis got a bad cut over his left eyelid from a headbutt. Dundee and cutman Chickie Ferrara went wild in Ellis's corner, calling for him to jab and move.

With half a minute remaining in round ten, the two men tangled up in a corner and exchanged left hooks. Ellis's got there first, and it brought Bonavena crashing into the corner where he appeared to huddle, almost cowering. His legs were gone, and he was lucky the knockdown happened when it did in the round; the bell rang and he recovered in the corner.

Suddenly inspired by the world-title shot disintegrating with each unanswered punch Ellis landed, Bonavena charged out of his corner for round eleven and attacked. Had Bonavena shown that kind of character more often, he would've had a different career, maybe even a different life. But it was too late; his punches had no power. Even with Ellis giving Dundee fits by lingering on the ropes, Bonavena couldn't take advantage.

Ellis hurt Bonavena again in the twelfth but inexplicably held him up, preventing him from falling to the canvas. It reflected that sparring-partner mentality, but Ellis still won the round and the fight by a relatively comfortable margin. One questionable judge, however, would have given the fight to Bonavena without the knockdowns.

Distraught, Bonavena wept between attempts at joking around and making light of his failure. In reality, this one stung. A world title was within reach and now it was gone.

A group of Argentine newsmen waited in Bonavena's dressing room as he sat on a chair in the shower reflecting on what just happened. Bonavena emerged from the shower and told everyone what they surely already knew by now: He would be taking a few months off and going home.

o o o

Reno newspapers said Joe Conforte moved to Los Angeles after being released from McNeil Island, but if that was true, he didn't stay long. Both Joe and Sally were in the news for a handful of things in 1966, none of them good.

In February, local law enforcement was called to the former site of a burned-down brothel owned by Sally when nearby residents reported gunfire. Sally and three men that sheriffs described as "well-known hoods" were seen coming from that direction and pulled over, whereupon a search of the car revealed an "arsenal" of at least three guns and a lot of ammunition. A few days later Sally was charged with operating a beauty salon without a license after being warned explicitly that she and Joe were no longer welcome in Reno.

Storey County District Attorney Robert Berry, a man well acquainted with Conforte and his capers, said Conforte moved back to the area in late May. Within days, Joe was arrested along with a bunch of workers from two of his brothels. Everyone arrested forfeited bail when they failed to show up for court.

Conforte was also arrested for assault with intent to kill in July, when one of his employees, a man named James H. Hrach, claimed Conforte and his associate Dick Lane beat him with a hose while holding a gun to his head. Court proceedings were abruptly halted in August, right around the same time that Conforte put an ad in local newspapers offering one year of paid rent and utilities at his new trailer park on the edge of town.

It was a game, with the district attorneys and law enforcement on one side and Conforte on the other. Some district attorney, often Berry, would raid one or more of Conforte's brothels or shake some of his girls down, and Conforte would deny any wrongdoing, charge officials with corruption through a newspaper, and then do something to spread his local influence. Berry's raids were increasing, though, and the trailer-park maneuver represented an escalation on Conforte's part.

"I am aware Conforte has bragged in Virginia City bars that he would pack enough voters into his end of the county to get me out of office," Berry told a *Nevada State Journal* reporter. Building a trailer park and packing it full of people whose votes he could buy meant he could vote out the officials he couldn't bribe.

"That district where I'm at, we have about three hundred voters," Conforte later told *Rolling Stone*. "I put in a trailer park for them, I put in an apartment house, and so on and so forth; and I'm more or less acquainted with those people. When it comes to voting, most of them vote the way I ask them to do. And this, by having those votes, it gives an advantage to the right guy in getting in."

But Conforte couldn't persuade everyone. Immediately after Conforte's assault proceedings were sidelined, he and Sally were ordered by a district judge to show cause why they continued selling sex despite countless law enforcement warnings and a recent court mandate. And rather than play by someone else's rules, Conforte simply adjusted his aim.

At the end of September of 1966, Conforte spoke to a packed Reno Press Club in the Riverside Hotel. He preached the benefits of prostitution and claimed he was in the business for the good of the community. Conforte even alluded to a murder he claimed never would have happened had the killer, a regular patron of a Conforte-owned brothel, been able to visit his establishments freely.

"[The murderer]'s what we call a freak," Conforte told the crowd of more than a hundred people, mostly women. "It's a harsh word but that's it. There's only two things that can be done with people like that—accommodate them or execute them." He went on to describe how the killer used to fake cutting his working girls with paper knives, which quenched his desire to actually take lives somehow. Conforte even brought a girl named Rita with him to back him up and silence doubters.

Rita told the crowd that prostitution allowed her to put her brothers and sisters through college, and that the higher pay meant they wouldn't have to struggle the way she did. When she said that she still expected to eventually settle down to raise a family, a woman in the crowd interrupted to exclaim, "That is not what will happen at all. You will be given to the Japanese fisherman, who will dump you in the ocean."

One reporter asked Rita if she knew how to swim. She responded, "You better believe it!"

Bill Farr, a Sparks fire chief who would go on to serve as a Nevada state senator, submitted a written complaint to the *Nevada State Journal* that said Conforte was being given free publicity by the Reno Press Club. Farr's complaint had little do with the prostitution itself—he objected to how Conforte framed politicians as "crooked" and corrupt at the press club appearance. Farr's status as a candidate for the U.S. Senate merited a response from the *Nevada State Journal*'s editor, who insisted Nevada residents ignore Conforte's words with "a kind of tongue-in-cheek curiosity and shrug of the shoulders."

It was an inadequate editor response to justifiable concern that Reno newspapers were allowing Conforte to spread his sex propaganda on their platforms unchallenged, and it painted Conforte as a harmless by-product of Nevada backcountry quirkiness. The rest of 1966 and just about all of 1967 should have indicated clearly that Conforte was worthy of shunning by Reno.

When two men, James Ing and Milton James Thompson, got arrested for murder and a string of other recent crimes in October, Conforte inexplicably attended their preliminary hearing at the Sparks Justice Court. More important, and somehow dismissed in newspapers, was the fact that a surviving witness claimed one of the accused killers mentioned Conforte just before one of the murders. Two weeks later, Conforte's accuser in the assault case, James Hrach, disappeared from protective custody and reportedly fled the country.

"Hrach was supposed to stay in a motel where we had put him," Berry said. "His disappearance from the country has left me no alternative but to drop the case."

Conforte could've just left the Reno area at any time. Starting fresh in some other city where he wasn't as notorious might've been a good idea. But Conforte had invested time and money into Reno and the surrounding small towns. Part of him probably felt pride that everyone from local toughs to law enforcement saw him as the mafia don of Reno. And ultimately if operating brothels and the capers that followed weren't profitable, he likely would've stopped.

Conforte stayed, however, and in February of 1967 a district judge named Richard Waters Jr. declared publicly that, "I want to keep Conforte out of business in Storey County." Waters revealed that the county spent $75 a day paying cops to stand guard near two known brothels and keep them closed.

James Ing was killed by gunfire from six officers during a sting two days after Waters's talk with newspapers. According to the police account, Ing agreed to sell undercover officers a stolen Pablo Picasso painting and some guns he'd acquired in a burglary a month earlier. They met in Reno, right in front of room number seven at the Stagecoach Inn, and when the cops sprung their trap and confronted an unarmed Ing, he threw the box of Picasso paintings at them and gestured as if reaching for a gun. They immediately opened fire and killed him. The pathologist at the Washoe Medical Center who performed the autopsy said Ing suffered "numerous and multiple penetrating missile wounds," and his cause of death ruled from "hemorrhaging and destruction of tissues."

The *Reno Gazette*'s news editor, Warren Lerude, wrote an article titled, "You a Criminal, Jimmy? Ing, Police Had Answers" the following day it served more as a good riddance letter than an obituary. Among the long list of Ing's sins was something easily overlooked: Ing served time at the Nevada State Prison with Conforte a few years earlier, and he claimed to run a blackjack game in the same gambling ring Conforte was also said to be involved in—the infamous "Bullpen." The so-called casino was actually an especially predatory system run by the roughest inmates, and it influenced Nevada lawmakers to introduce a bill banning gambling in maximum security prisons.

Once again under legal scrutiny and with apparent associates of his facing serious issues, the world looked to be closing in on Conforte, just as it had when he got caught trying to extort Washoe County District Attorney Bill Raggio in 1959. That's what sent him to state prison in the first place, until it snowballed into a yearslong bid for various charges. Returning to the sex business after being released was risky and foolish but Conforte did it anyway, never publicly showing much doubt about his ventures. This time wouldn't be any different.

In early March of 1967, Conforte was called before a federal grand jury linked to a probe on "white slavery," a racially charged concept meant to distinguish regular old prostitution from sex trafficking. In this case, Conforte and an associate were suspected of transporting a woman across state lines, from California to Nevada, to work in one of his brothels. Days later, injunctions from a district court judge ordered Conforte to close both of his local brothels and pay back the money Storey County had spent paying deputies to guard them.

Conforte quickly made the first $1,000 payment of the $5,000 total. As always, he kept up appearances, cooperating just enough to divert attention from his usual slippery tactics. Nobody knew it at that point, but one of Conforte's next moves would eventually lead to Oscar Bonavena's death.

A board meeting involving local commissioners of Washoe and Storey Counties in May 1967 centered its discussion on one thing: the attention that a brothel across the nearby Truckee River kept drawing. The Mustang River Ranch opened in 1964 in an area east of Reno known as the "River District". Recently law enforcement posted deputies to guard this brothel location too, which meant that anyone driving in that direction could be stopped and questioned. The ethics of prostitution weren't the primary concern, so much as the prudence of spending the county's finances on the problem of another county.

Nevertheless issues surrounding Mustang became a serious concern for the first time. That was when Conforte stepped in and took over the brothel, renaming it Mustang Bridge Ranch, or Mustang Ranch for short. That was the name of the place Oscar Bonavena's demise. would be linked to forever.

○ ○ ○

The heavyweight tournament didn't look to be turning much of a profit because most of the money was going to substantial fighter guarantees. Bonavena alone got $50,000 for Mildenberger and $75,000 for Ellis. The German claimed a portion of ticket sales, Bonavena the foreign television rights, and the Louisville gate flopped.

That didn't matter to Bonavena. When he was back at home, he had his wife and daughter plus several sources of income, such as a barbershop and a nightclub. As long as the money flowed his way, everyone else was on their own.

But, true to his word, Bonavena returned to the ring in February and March of 1968 against overmatched opponents. Sometime during the March bout he aggravated his back injury, and a few days later the contract with Goldberg expired. It was then that a familiar name popped up.

Lee Carr never quite sustained his amateur success in the pro ranks. As Bonavena bounced back and forth between continents, Carr brought his record to 8-4, even managing to fight on a few Madison Square Garden cards and once at the Boston Garden. The four losses all came against the only significant opponents he'd faced. Following a few months off in 1967, he was scheduled for a May showdown against Leotis Martin in Philadelphia. Carr and Martin actually fought in the same 1961 Intercity Golden Gloves tournament with Jimmy Ellis. How different their fates had all been.

When Madison Square Garden approached Carr to sign him for a grudge match against Bonavena, back when the two were still undefeated, he refused outright. Carr made his own way in the sport, without a Goldman, Goldberg, or a syndicate propping him up. By 1967, however, Lee and his wife had children and needed money. Carr already had vision problems and was out of shape but boxing paid the bills.

"When I fought Leotis Martin," Carr told a reporter about a year before his death in 2008, "I couldn't see none of his punches. That's why I got pounded to death."

Martin dropped Carr with a left-right combination in the opening round, and Carr wobbled to his corner at the bell. A hook dropped him again in round two, and then a right hand flattened him for the count moments later. Realizing he was likely through, Carr did what any real boxer does: He kept fighting anyway.

A call came from Luna Park offering Carr a chance to add a pro win over Bonavena to his 1963 Pan Am Games victory. Luna Park proposed a $5,000 purse to take on Bonavena at the famed venue. It was Carr's biggest purse to date. Realistically, he had no choice.

Sadly, there was also no chance. On April 20, 1968, still carrying the same spare tire around his waist that he had against Martin eleven months earlier, Carr's bad eyesight ensured he saw even fewer punches coming. Two of them, a pair of left hooks to the liver, dropped Carr for the count in round three following a strange body-shot knockdown.

Horrific body shots typically cause fighters to take a knee, but Carr's legs stopped working altogether and went stiff. He fell awkwardly onto his back and didn't have the strength to hoist himself up before being counted out.

Nothing that happened since Bonavena bit Carr could be undone, but, in winning, he made up for his biggest boxing misdeed to date. Besides, changing his destiny would have required a level of introspection Bonavena simply hadn't shown.

Bonavena had vengeance against Frazier and Folley on his mind, and Luna Park representatives reached out to George Parnassus, the legendary matchmaker and promoter at the Olympic Auditorium, about booking George "Scrap Iron" Johnson for Bonavena at the Olympic in July. Johnson had recently gone rounds with Frazier, so people expected a similar performance against Bonavena. Unsurprisingly, Bonavena quietly signed a contract to face Folley too close to the proposed date for Johnson in Los Angeles, which pissed off Parnassus.

Only two years had passed since Bonavena's first defeat. But the time from thirty-five to thirty-seven had affected Folley; he'd been knocked out by Ali and trudged through several other fights and his record was

2-1-2 in his last five bouts before he met this old foe. In *The Ring*, where he recently held a number-one ranking, Folley's name disappeared because of losses and his failing to face real contenders.

A 5-to-3 favorite, Bonavena took a majority decision win, with one Argentine judge voting for a draw and the other two handing the fight to their man. Despite getting wobbled twice by Folley's shots, Bonavena kept the pressure on Folley, who wilted in the last few rounds and couldn't sustain any offense. The 25,000 spectators at Luna Park booed the decision loudly anyway, and Bonavena walked away from the fight with a chronic hand injury. Another night that was supposed to have been a grand triumph for Bonavena ended with both insult and injury.

Back in the United States, Jimmy Ellis won the WBA's vacant title by soundly defeating Jerry Quarry via decision. Ali, still widely imitated, remained out of action, and the NYSAC chose to make Frazier their heavyweight champion. As the International Boxing Club of New York proved fifteen years earlier, controlling the heavyweight title meant substantial influence in boxing in addition to the potential for producing cash.

Split claims to the championship meant only Frazier against Ellis could decide supremacy without Ali. The various entities with financial stakes and investments needed to meet and get the fight scheduled. In the meantime, both men still had to fight. The entire situation was a disaster at heavyweight. Somehow there were two champions, neither of them Ali. It was a cynical power vacuum. Glory was there for someone to take, just not Bonavena.

Historically, most dark-skinned fighters who dared to pursue success in boxing were treated as exotic sideshows. If they ran the gauntlet and survived, they were then treated as if they attempted to overthrow the structure of American sports. From the reign of Jack Johnson—boxing's first black heavyweight champion—up until 1968, little had changed.

Joe Frazier knew racism. He had dark skin, rough hair, and often spoke with a Southern drawl. Born in Beaufort, South Carolina, Frazier left for New York after several incidents with local whites forced him to reassess his prospects in the South.

Cloverlay Inc.'s investment in Frazier's career made him more easily visible, in a business sense. White businessmen have owned most fighters since boxing began, but Cloverlay, Inc., with over five hundred investors, was different. There were clergy members, teachers, and bankers among them, and they were mostly white businesspeople. A lot of them. Years later Cloverlay would grow to over a thousand investors. Sportswriter Larry Merchant even bought one share at $250 just for fun, and sold it later for $2,000.

Muhammad Ali, largely bankrolled by the Nation of Islam, would memorably push his nose in, make gorilla noises, and call Frazier "Uncle Tom" before their three fights. Receiving career funding from a battery of investors, almost all of them white, became just one more thing for Ali to torment Frazier about.

In the two years and ten fights since he narrowly beat Bonavena in 1966, Frazier won back confidence in his chin by defeating the likes of George Chuvalo, Doug Jones, and Manuel Ramos. None were big punchers but neither was Bonavena, and he had whacked Frazier to the canvas twice and almost won.

Thankfully, it looked like Frazier's chin wasn't the liability his backers feared. And nobody doubted Frazier's heart or grit.

Lou Lucchese, a toy store owner involved in Frazier's career early on, brainstormed the idea of getting Bonavena to Frazier's adopted home of Philadelphia for a rematch. In September, shortly after Bonavena beat Leotis Martin in Buenos Aires, Lucchese told reporters he would soon have enough money to secure rights to the rematch and intended to fly to Argentina and convince Bonavena personally.

Amid everyone else's maneuvering, Bonavena at least stayed busy, appearing at Luna Park four times in just over five months, including the Martin fight. The Rago brothers put up with Bonavena's nonsense in the gym, perhaps because of the Parque Patricios connection, but they'd probably at least acknowledged how Bonavena discarded others he didn't need.

Two things Bonavena did need, however, were Luna Park and Tito Lectoure. In an unprecedented move, Lectoure conceded a portion of television rights to Bonavena. He also allowed Bonavena to fight for a percentage of the gate receipts rather than a fixed purse. This permissive approach toward handling Bonavena, while groundbreaking from a fighter's perspective, backfired thoroughly. Acquiescing to Bonavena's demands and keeping him comfortable just made him grab for more. When asked if the Garden would pursue the Frazier–Bonavena rematch, their boxing director Harry Markson said, "[Bonavena] wants too much."

Madison Square Garden had dealt with Bonavena before, however. They knew he was difficult. Lucchese had no clue, or else he wouldn't have flown to Buenos Aires and romanced Bonavena with a purse offer of $75,000 tax-free. He wouldn't have dogged Bonavena for three days, begging him to sign.

Bonavena wouldn't relent until Lucchese promised that Frank Sinatra, the patron saint of the Bonavena household, would be sitting ringside at the Philadelphia Spectrum. Even after all of that, Bonavena insisted on taking one more fight at Luna Park first. He got one of the biggest stars in show business as his personal guest and still wanted more.

"Don't you think I'm eating my heart out 'til that's over?" Lucchese sweated to the press at a luncheon announcing the Frazier–Bonavena rematch. Thankfully, Bonavena needed just over one minute to level "Big" Jim Fletcher for the count with a hook. Bonavena then traveled to the United States intent on wiping out an American star, as he had three times before.

Bonavena brought his wife, Dora, and their children along for the Frazier rematch. And Bonavena's brother José estimated that between thirty and forty family members as well as friends who'd also traveled to support Ringo occupied three suites at Philadelphia's Benjamin Franklin Motor Inn.

The week of the fight, Frazier and Bonavena met at the Spectrum for their prefight physical exams. Always the talker, Bonavena stole the show by putting his plump fist under Joe's chin and asking, "Remember this?" Everything was fun—until Bonavena's mood turned serious.

It's possible Bonavena was simply amusing himself and didn't mean serious harm. Maybe when he acted out, he just wanted a reaction—any reaction. But when Frazier playfully grabbed at Bonavena's bicep, the air left the room. Bonavena stopped and pointed scoldingly, saying through his interpreter George Wila that if he were touched again the fight would be off.

Apart from not wanting his food or clothes messed with, Bonavena didn't like to be touched. It made no sense. Bonavena would reach out to smack, jostle, throttle, or push just about anyone on a whim. He nearly killed an elderly Charley Goldman tripping him for fun a few years earlier. Yet he himself didn't like to be touched.

In his time, writers dismissed Bonavena's conduct and called him a clown. It was true, too; he was playful and loved to make people laugh. It just wasn't all games. Behind the jokes was a bully and an antagonist—and he was headed in the wrong direction.

Frazier trained in the Philadelphia gym purchased for him by Cloverlay while Bonavena worked out with Hector Nesci, his latest trainer, across the river at Paul Fleck's Pro Am Gym in Camden, New Jersey.

Bonavena and his team couldn't find anyone to stand and trade with him in sparring as they expected Frazier to on fight night. Roy "Tiger" Williams, a shifty, unbeaten heavyweight and former Golden Gloves champion, was called away from his day job to spar with Bonavena, who disrespectfully showed up very late. So Williams made Bonavena chase him, moved his head a lot, and countered Bonavena to hell. Bonavena was furious. After four rounds of not being able to catch Williams clean, Bonavena walked to the ropes and attempted to dislodge them violently out of frustration.

Leotis Martin flew in at the last minute for a few days' work and Nesci, Wila, and Bonavena complained they'd found nothing but "runners" to spar. But the sparring partners weren't the issue. Between Bonavena and Frazier, one fighter was on a path to immortality and the other was going to lose and go home. That's how it happened three times before.

There was a sort of peace in Bonavena's family life. In Buenos Aires, family gatherings were not only expected, but on holidays they were actually covered by the Argentine press. Women would crowd the kitchen and family members put out big table spreads in the Bonavena living room. Children ran around as reporters tried to ask Bonavena questions.

In fact, Oscar was often surrounded by groups of kids, and easily overlooked among prefight predictions and oddsmaker breakdowns of the Frazier fight were photos of Bonavena and Adriana. They danced for reporters. Adriana climbed atop his head and screamed with glee as he rode her tiny tricycle. They played records and snuggled up on the motel couch. Maybe that was the real Bonavena, but being crass was too profitable.

Oddsmakers suspected what would happen against Frazier, making him a strong favorite over Bonavena at anywhere from 2-to-1 to 3-to-1. Fighting in his adopted hometown could have been a factor, but, just as likely, observers simply didn't know whether to take Bonavena seriously or to laugh him off—even if he did have a 38-4 record.

More important, the tough Philadelphia gym scene and rigorous training regimen pushed the 21-0 Frazier toward the elite level. At five feet eleven and with only moderate reach, Frazier's style was a product of physical limitations, but he stifled, pushed, muscled, and hooked his way to victories over taller, stronger, and more skilled opponents. Bonavena only had strength on Frazier, and that's overrated in boxing.

The day of the fight, December 10, 1968, Muhammad Ali barked to a small crowd in front of the Spectrum that a false heavyweight-title defense would be happening inside. He still went in and attended. So did boxing royalty like Jack Dempsey, Rocky Marciano, Sugar Ray Robinson, and old light heavyweight stylist Tommy Loughran. There were also celebrities in attendance like Ed Sullivan, Miles Davis, and Frankie Avalon. And Frank Sinatra was there, as Lucchese promised.

During the fight, Bonavena jabbed well initially and countered Frazier with uppercuts and hooks. Yet, inexplicably, he resorted to holding his gloves high to the sides of his head and sitting with his back to the ropes, and Frazier gladly took what was given to him.

The fight was actually a surprising display of trench warfare, even from Bonavena. Both fighters bombed at each other in close, often straying low and using forearms and shoulders to create space. Frazier outgunned and outworked Bonavena consistently, but he took punishment for his effort. Only four pounds separated them, with Frazier weighing 203 pounds and Bonavena 207.

Several times the fighters mixed it up after the bell because they couldn't hear it ring over the clamor of Argentine fans banging drums. Bonavena, who typically showed good stamina, looked like he felt the pressure as he walked to his corner after rounds four and five. In round six, Frazier's hostility grew. He found the range and angle on his left hook and slammed a few home. Halfway through the round, a headbutt opened up a bad cut on Bonavena's right eye.

As the round ended, a small man with a dark toupee and cotton-tipped applicators in his mouth rushed through the ropes and grabbed Bonavena by the arm, leading him to his stool. Adolph Ritacco, a well-known Philly trainer and cutman who'd been an undefeated bantamweight decades earlier, had been tasked with fixing Bonavena's face. Before long there were cuts on Bonavena's left eye and nose too.

Both men caught each other with low blows, though only Bonavena got penalized. The Argentine lost the eighth round on a low-blow penalty. If he wanted to take the Philadelphia champion's title in his hometown, his chances waned as the fight went on.

"Come on, Oscar," Joe kept saying in the clinch. "Mix it. Mix it up. Ain't got nothin'."

The bell sounded for the tenth round and again Sweeney couldn't hear it. Bonavena fell back into a corner and Frazier went straight to work, banging away. Yank Durham actually rammed his arm through the ropes to cover up Bonavena, protecting him from his own fighter. Lost in the action was the fact that Frazier had grown tired from laying a beating on Bonavena and, to be fair, the punches he had to walk through.

Over the next five rounds, Bonavena showed about as much heart and courage as he ever would. He fought his way off the ropes, met Frazier in the center of the ring, and swelled up Frazier's face.

Bonavena won the final three rounds on Sweeney's card yet fell well short of capturing any of the cards. Frazier walked away with the unanimous decision win, a puffy face, and his five-state heavyweight title.

Frazier sat in his dressing room with a bag of ice on the right side of his face for a while before talking to reporters. Bonavena visited as soon as he could and apologized for the low blows.

"I'll be champion when you die," Oscar told him.

"You'll be waiting a long time," Frazier replied.

Goldberg, who had driven in from New York for the fight, flashed his manager's badge to get backstage and went to Bonavena's dressing room. George Wila punched him in the mouth and tossed him out.

The day after the fight, Bonavena's cutman Adolph Ritacco let slip that he was fired from Bonavena's corner minutes before the fight began because Bonavena didn't want to pay the $100 fee. Nesci and others convinced Bonavena to rehire him, but Ritacco wasn't allowed into the ring unless there was a cut. That's why Ritacco bounded into the ring seemingly out of nowhere when Bonavena's skin split.

Lou Lucchese hoped for around 12,000 spectators and a $300,000 gate to make the show profitable. Instead, around 8,000 showed up for a bit over $200,000. The toy store owner took a huge financial hit, and it wasn't over. As Bonavena hightailed it back to Buenos Aires, the IRS filed a tax lien against him for over $63,000. Lucchese handed over a copy of a contract stating Bonavena would be paid $25,000, one-third of the purse he publicly demanded and was reportedly promised. Something didn't add up. For some reason Lucchese then stepped in and pledged to pay whatever taxes Bonavena owed.

Bonavena didn't make a clean getaway back to Argentina this time. As he and Frazier battled, someone broke into the suites at the Franklin Motor Inn and stole television sets and stereos the Bonavenas planned to take home.

Bonavena wrangled money out of so many people that everyone had a motive to rob him. If he wasn't demanding cash outright, he was wasting money by refusing to train or taking equipment with him back to Buenos Aires and "losing" it. How long could his act stave off what he had coming?

"[Oscar] does a great pantomime of the great fighters: Clay, Patterson, Liston," Marvin Goldberg once said. "And then someone asks him, Do you speak English? He says, 'Sure. $60,000, $70,000, $80,000. . . .'"

o o o

Bonavena once told a story about how he got his nickname. According to Carlos Irusta, author and longtime writer for *El Gráfico,* Bonavena told him that he encountered a group of teens who saw him as he was leaving a hotel in New York during his first visit to the United States. They yelled "Ringo!" at him and he decided to roll with it.

It's impossible to know whether to believe the story, great as it may be. It's no more outlandish than some of boxing's enduring urban legends, however. On paper, it was New York *Daily News* writer Dick Young who first referred to Bonavena as "Ringo." His article, "Ringo of the Ring," featured a cartoon of Bonavena appearing to fall forward while clumsily throwing a punch, drawn by artist Bill Gallo.

Both Young and Gallo bought shares in Bonavena's earlier syndicate IT&T. Both were well acquainted with Harry Markson, who at that point had more than twenty years of experience at the Garden, and Charlie Johnston, the manager whose two-way deal with Luna Park opened the door for Bonavena to visit the United States in the first place.

Frankly, it's just as likely the "Ringo" thing was an invention and coordinated effort to sell Bonavena to the public. In any case it's no wonder

Bonavena crooned Beatles tunes, and it makes sense that he would mimic Ali's boxing rhymes, predict the round he'd win by knockout, and so on. There was money in copying these ridiculously popular figures, and it was the pop culture Bonavena was inundated by during his first trip to the United States.

On February 7, 1964, thousands of Americans besieged the Kennedy International Airport as the Beatles arrived in the United States. Even more people followed their every move through New York City that day by listening to a local radio broadcast. Two days later, seventy-three million people watched the band make their U.S. television debut on *The Ed Sullivan Show*. As the band filmed a second appearance on the show in Miami a week later, publicist Harold Conrad arranged a meeting between then-heavyweight title challenger Cassius Clay and the Beatles at the 5th Street Gym.

The braggadocio of a young, good-looking talent like Ali overshadowed a surly, bland Liston, who the boxing world nevertheless recognized as its premier big man for a time. For years a Liston scowl and pose was even part of Bonavena's repertoire of impersonations—possibly the easiest one.

Bonavena expressed interest in fighting Liston several times and might have gotten the chance had he defeated Frazier in the rematch. In 1968, wrestling promoter Vince McMahon Sr. guaranteed Bonavena either $150,000 or 25 percent of the gate receipts of a Liston fight should he defeat Frazier. But Bonavena's money problems grew to a size he could no longer manage with jokes. He'd lost the big fight again, and when he returned to Buenos Aires this time he found his businesses crumbling. If that wasn't enough, he found out he owed back taxes in Argentina too. Authorities then claimed Bonavena's $2,000 purse for his first fight back from the Frazier loss, against Brazilian Luis Faustino Pires in March of 1969 in Mar de Plata, south of Buenos Aires.

Presumably to avoid taxes, Bonavena flew to Berlin in May and fought Wilhelm Von Homburg in June, but the whole thing almost fell apart because of Bonavena's usual antics. He threatened to pull out more than once, citing inadequate training quarters and small sparring partners, before getting sick and postponing the fight twice while already in Berlin with Dora. The German newspaper *Bild* suggested that Bonavena wasn't actually sick but using illness as an excuse to press for more money.

Interestingly Von Homburg was more actor and celebrity than legitimate fighter; he grew his hair long and the German press called him "The Beatle Boxer." Bonavena sent him to the canvas five times before stopping him in three rounds.

The postponement in Germany forced Bonavena to abandon plans to fight in Italy beforehand, which also pushed back a scheduled third fight against Peralta in Uruguay. This time Peralta and Bonavena fought to a draw as the latter turned out a poor performance. Goyo looked younger than his thirty-four years and used loose ropes to avoid most of Bonavena's rushes.

"What we can openly maintain is that Bonavena was at 30 percent of what he is and what he could do [against Peralta]," wrote Horacio García Blanco in the Argentine magazine *Goles*. The draw vaulted Peralta into the world heavyweight rankings as Bonavena simply maintained the top-ten ranking he'd kept for most of the last two years.

When Bonavena returned to Argentina to face Santiago Alberto Lovell, an Olympian, former professional *fútbol* player, and the son of a 1932 Argentine Olympic gold medal boxer of the same name, Oscar was supposed to be on his best behavior. His relationship with Lectoure grew strained following years of the manager's unsuccessful attempts at advising him.

"Oscar wanted to do whatever he wanted to do, and he didn't like anyone coming around and telling him what to do," Vicente Bonavena later told writer Ezequiel Fernández Moores. "But those were normal fights Oscar had with Tito."

Instead of acting civilized, Bonavena laid into Lovell at the weigh-in, threatening to shoot him. According to Juan Manuel Bordón and Guido Carelli Lynch in *Luna Park: El Estadio del Pueblo, El Ring del Poder*, Bonavena also resorted to racist outbursts toward a dark-skinned opponent, which he'd done before and would do again. Later that night, Bonavena forced officials to stop the fight after Lovell got pummeled for eight rounds.

In January Bonavena fought for the first time in 1970, having serious difficulty with smaller veteran Miguel Angel Paez through five rounds, and getting hit with a series of right hands by Paez in round six that staggered him. The Luna Park crowd cheered on Bonavena's punishment. In round seven Bonavena relied on an old trick and hit Paez low. It backfired. Unable to continue, Paez was given the win on a foul while Bonavena shook his gloves angrily at his opponent and officials. Paez never gave Bonavena the chance to avenge the loss, openly refusing a rematch.

Bonavena fought Alberto Lovell again and trounced him at Luna Park in March of 1970, knocking him down five times and putting him away in nine rounds. Wins over José Humberto Menno, "Pulgarcito" Manuel Ramos, and James Woody came next.

Three things happened while Bonavena remained in South America this time. First, a young former Olympian named George Foreman emerged as a force in the division. Second, the Beatles officially broke up. And finally, Muhammad Ali was granted a license to fight in Georgia, thanks to the wrangling of State Senator Leroy Johnson.

Bonavena rose to the top spot in the WBA's heavyweight rankings in September of 1970. That same month several newspapers floated rumors that Ali could fight Bonavena in Miami at some point. Another former champion, Floyd Patterson, suggested Bonavena as a prospective opponent too.

In late October, just as Bonavena announced that he would be facing old foe Luis Faustino Pires at Luna Park, he also said he would be facing the winner of Muhammad Ali vs. Jerry Quarry, which was just days away. Bonavena predicted Ali would win, and he was right.

During a later training session for the Pires fight at Luna Park, a reporter told Bonavena that Pires said he'd improved since their first two bouts and asked Oscar if he agreed. Bonavena replied, "I don't think [Pires] can withstand much. He said he's gotten better, that he's changed. . . ." A silly grin fell over his face, and he finished his thought, saying, "Well, he's blacker [now]!"

o o o

Joe Conforte seemingly had a race issue of his own back in Reno: "White slavery" charges initiated in 1967 stuck with him through the year. In April, Conforte testified in a U.S. District Court case of a Louisiana man charged with bringing his ex-wife from New Orleans to Reno for sex work. The following month Conforte and his wife Sally were charged with operating a brothel out of a local motel; and in June, Conforte was charged with transporting a woman from California to Nevada to work for him.

The Mann Act, passed by Congress nearly sixty years earlier, was the result of a commission appointed to investigate "white slavery," or forced prostitution. Lawmakers argued no woman would ever enter into prostitution by choice, though the Mann Act was often used as an excuse to enforce laws based on skin color. In 1912, for example, Jack Johnson was charged with bringing a white prostitute, who was actually his wife, across state lines from Pittsburgh to Chicago.

White slavery was a misguided and antiquated concept, but crossing state lines while committing crimes is still a great way to get the attention of the feds. The man with whom Conforte was charged, George Perry, aka George Piscitelle, also had their attention years earlier for his associations.

In the late 1950s, Perry regularly hung around Los Angeles crime boss Mickey Cohen. In fact, Perry was seated at a dinner table with Cohen when a friend of theirs named Sam Lo Cigno shot and killed "The Enforcer" Jack Whalen at a restaurant on Ventura Boulevard. "'Biggest Bookie' in Valley Slain," read the *Los Angeles Times* headline the following day. Perry was booked alongside three others and charged with murder and conspiracy. Perry, Cohen, and the fourth man, Joe De Carlo, were all acquitted and released while Lo Cigno, the shooter, ate the charge and did prison time.

Though Nevada newspaper reports didn't mention it at the time, Perry was also one of the "well-known hoods" in the car when Sally Conforte was pulled over and disarmed eighteen months earlier. An article from the *San Francisco Examiner* explained that Sally was attempting to reenter the old site of her burned trailer when a voice from the darkness said, "Come through and we'll blow your guts out," before a shotgun blast rang through the hills. The same article named Perry.

These criminal associations and misadventures kept Conforte's name in Reno newspapers throughout 1967. Apart from his prison time for extortion and tax evasion, Conforte had managed to escape trouble most of the time, either conveniently getting charges dropped or having scandals fade away. But Conforte's master strategy to confound authorities by operating at the intersection of four different Nevada counties backfired. Sheriff's deputies and district attorneys from each county spent too much time either sniffing out or smoothing over Conforte's vice dealing. It became too noticeable. Conforte's antics weren't just local news anymore, and policing him, even if only superficially, ate into taxpayer money. Conforte couldn't bribe or scheme quickly enough to stay ahead for long.

Conforte spent a few days in jail before petitioning for and receiving a bail reduction. Shortly after being released, he confronted a former associate alongside three others and may have been stabbed or cut in a scuffle, though he denied it to a Reno newspaper.

When Conforte went to Las Vegas in September, he was arrested by local deputies and charged with failing to register as an ex-felon. The twenty-one-year-old woman he was with caught a vagrancy charge. The message that Conforte wasn't welcome in Vegas couldn't have been clearer.

The year finished with Conforte being hit with a tax lien, losing an effort to have his white slavery case dismissed, and being named as a "go-between" in a *San Francisco Examiner* article about a double murder in a suspected Nevada killing-for-hire ring, which was somehow never again talked about.

His white slavery trial finished in January of 1968 about as quickly as it began, however. A young former prostitute named Champagne testified about being trafficked between Reno and Los Angeles to turn tricks and the strict, oppressive schedules working girls kept. Conforte and

Perry were acquitted when the district judge said the state failed to prove its case and Conforte, persecution complex on full display, loudly bluffed to newspapers that he'd be leaving the state permanently because of his recent court treatment.

He didn't leave Nevada. How could he? Conforte had been there more than a decade and invested time and money into carving out his slice of sagebrush heaven. Conforte's desert oasis was a trailer complex in the dry, sandy hills, a palatial trailer park of young prostitutes. Legal threats wouldn't dissuade Conforte, but they did quiet him down for most of 1968.

In May, George Perry was killed in what papers called a "Gangland-Style Shooting" in a Van Nuys, California, apartment complex, ending that association entirely. But in December, Mustang Ranch caught fire. The damage was estimated at $100,000. "There's no use crying about it," Conforte told his girls as they huddled under blankets and sobbed watching their clothes burn in the blaze.

Conforte never stayed quiet for long. He was like Bonavena that way. Wherever they went, they were disruptive. People looked at them and people talked about them. Rivals didn't like them. In Conforte's case, rivals *really* didn't like him—to the point of trying to blow up his house.

After receiving a tip in March of 1969, Washoe County deputies arrested two men with a trunk full of dynamite before they could carry out their plan to destroy Conforte's house. One of the men, Donald Baliotis, was charged with possessing a dynamite machine and attempting to use dynamite to blow up an unoccupied building, receiving an extremely light punishment of four years of probation. Likely recognizing an opportunity to capitalize off his newfound victimhood, Conforte made a far bolder move in June of 1969: he went after the Reno bus lines.

The Reno bus line declared bankruptcy and Conforte put in a bid to run Reno's buses. "I would do it strictly as a goodwill gesture to the community," Conforte said to the *Reno Gazette*. "Reno has been good to me and maybe I could do something for the poor people of Reno, the ones who cannot afford to take a taxi."

The next year of Conforte's life was spent in countless meetings and hearings, filing paperwork, amending applications, and attempting to convince the people of Reno that he could run its public transportation in good faith. Citizens of Reno wrote letters to editors in support of and opposing Conforte's bid; editors answered. Conforte suggested a public vote by newspaper ballot on the issue and emerged victorious at 14-1. The *Reno Gazette* took a hard-line stance against the idea—as did Reno's mayor Roy Bankofier—but their resistance nor the hurdles Nevada's Public Service Commission kept putting in Conforte's way didn't deter him. He was tenacious. The PSC said Conforte had the wrong kinds of buses, so he came up with money for the correct kind. When the PSC brought up Conforte's criminal background, he responded that he'd done his prison time and since served his community, and indeed he'd mostly stayed out of trouble for months this time.

In March of 1970, shortly after being featured in an issue of *Newsweek*, Mustang Ranch was raided and found to not only be serving alcohol without a license, but pushing the illegal drinks on customers as a way to get the girls extra tips. It went downhill for Conforte from there. In April, a taxi driver was found murdered on the road just outside Conforte's Mustang brothel, and in May a group of prominent Nevada businessmen spoke out publicly about Conforte's bus line bid. And in June, a new bid on the bus lines was placed by the more experienced Nevada Transit Co.

Resilient as Conforte was, too many forces were against him on this one. A "mild heart attack" put Conforte in the hospital for a week, prompting his official bus company, JC Bus Lines, to shuffle its leadership around. The PSC then officially rejected Conforte's bid to take over Reno's bus lines in August.

Immediately following the verdict, one of the candidates for an upcoming vote for Washoe County district attorney accused the other of showing favoritism to Conforte, who as usual feigned surprise and denied everything. The weeklong exchange in the newspapers renewed the discussion surrounding the legalization of prostitution in Nevada, which was basically just a debate about Conforte, and when someone shone a light into that dark corner, they almost never liked what they found.

When Conforte was called to testify during the trial of the man accused of killing the taxi driver found dead outside of Mustang Ranch, his testimony confirmed what kind of operation he ran. Conforte said he noticed the taxi driver's car parked near Mustang and ordered a guard to check things out. When the guard found the driver's body and reported back, Conforte told the guard to wipe prints off of the car door handle.

A California man named John Lee Layton was found to have robbed and killed the driver, but the taxi was symbolic of Conforte's true motive behind the bus bid: local cops had been cracking down on taxi drivers who took men from Reno to the brothel and Conforte needed reliable transportation for clientele. It probably wasn't coincidence that transportation unions, which usually came packaged with transportation companies, had long been infiltrated by mob figures in 1970. Historically, the Greco Mafia in Calabria and Sicily owned a bus company and controlled transportation in the area. At worst, Conforte, born in Augusta, Sicily, would have known of the Greco Mafia before he left for the United States at eleven or twelve. He made regular trips back to Sicily, though, donating to a church and walking the older, cobblestone parts of his hometown like a big shot.

Wherever the bus idea truly came from, it was gone and Conforte needed a new angle, a new way to win over Reno. So he turned, at least briefly, to another mob favorite: boxing.

On one of his trips to Italy, Conforte tried to convince middleweight champion Nino Benvenuti, a native of Trieste, to visit Reno and defend his title there. Benvenuti lost the championship to Carlos Monzon later in 1970, but by then Conforte's efforts were overshadowed by one of boxing's titans anyway.

Boxing wasn't nonexistent in Reno, but it wasn't a fight town either. One of the few local fight figures was a member of the Nevada Athletic Commission named Bud Traynor. A known local businessman, he also owned a gas station in town. Traynor offered to co-promote an upcoming fight between Muhammad Ali and Oscar Bonavena with Chris Dundee, brother of Ali's trainer Angelo. Dundee told Reno reporters he liked the city's chances of landing the fight because it wouldn't eat into closed-circuit sales. Ultimately Reno lost its chance to Madison Square Garden when the Nevada Athletic Commission's chairman upheld a prior decision not to license Ali as punishment for his draft-evasion conviction. For once it had nothing to do with Conforte.

Bonavena needed a fight against Ali more than ever at the end of 1970. Not for his ego or for the sake of defeating the deposed champion, but because he needed the payday.

Another win over Pires allowed Bonavena to focus on the Ali fight, which he promoted as well as he could. On the street in Buenos Aires, an interviewer asked Bonavena what he thought about Ali as a rival, and Bonavena said, "I have a big advantage: I'm white and I'm from Argentina." While it's possible Bonavena failed to understand the social climate in the United States, it's just as likely, if not more so, that he understood exactly what he was doing and the damage it did. More than once he called himself "the great white hope of Argentina." The term directly referenced Jack Johnson's struggle for respect in a white boxing establishment, and Bonavena used it to mock Ali's predicament.

The FAB, tired of Bonavena's nonsense, pulled his license citing a refusal to cut his hair and continued uncouth behavior. They were legitimate gripes, but the FAB was probably also annoyed that Bonavena kept threatening to never fight in Argentina again. Luna Park honchos couldn't have appreciated such talk either.

Ali's trainer and manager, Angelo Dundee, brought Jimmy Ellis to Argentina to fight Goyo Peralta in 1969 only for the fight to be canceled at the last moment. Dundee's friend, Argentine promoter Héctor Méndez, put the fight card together and Méndez promoted Bonavena's bout with Peralta in Montevideo. From a business standpoint, these previous dealings likely made Ali–Bonavena easy to finalize. Once again Bonavena was the only thing standing in the way of his own progress.

Several major cities in the United States wanted the money and notoriety that came with hosting an Ali fight, and the Garden reluctantly entered the competition, knowing full well what kind of issues Bonavena typically brought with him.

In the balance hung a potential $10 million fight between Ali and Joe Frazier, who held the title many felt Ali rightly deserved to still possess. A number like $10 million dollars, even in 1970, was nearly unfathomable as fight revenue. Jack Dempsey and Georges Carpentier brought in the first million-dollar gate (and then some) in 1921, but through fifty years there had still been a cap on how much any fight could conceivably make. Ali risked eight figures fighting Bonavena.

The Argentine flew to New York in early November to renew his boxing license and along the way recruited New York trainer Gil Clancy to work with him for the Ali fight. "Let me put it this way," Clancy told the New York *Daily News*, "if I was managing Ali and I was presented with a list of opponents, the first name I'd cross off would be that of Bonavena."

Why? Because Ali never learned to fight inside, Clancy said. And for all the greatness, for all the rhyming and the stories and good looks, Ali couldn't fight with his back to the ropes. Not *really* fight, anyway. He could stall, hold, spin an opponent in the opposite direction or push, but he couldn't plant his feet and dig body shots. He didn't want to go to war.

For all of Bonavena's unflattering qualities both in the ring and out, he had moxie when punches flew his way. In the clinch it meant foes better brace their body for punishment.

Ali called Bonavena "Beast" and teased him through the press for his lack of skill. A press gathering at the Garden was the perfect opportunity for the Argentine to respond, and he did by calling Ali "black kangaroo."

Bonavena set up training camp in San Juan, Puerto Rico, telling the press he'd be moving there. When he made the final trip to New York, he returned to his old home at Grossinger's and brought with him a herd of teammates, supporters, and more—never a great sign for the unworthy.

Ali had an entourage, yes. But he was Ali. Sugar Ray Robinson had an entourage, but that was the Greatest of All Time. This was Ringo Bonavena.

Among Bonavena's group were co-managers he picked up specifically for when he was in Puerto Rico, José Montano and Hiram Cuevas, both of whom had money to front the fighter; the Rago brothers, his sometimes-trainers; a conditioner, Lopez Aguidar; his personal doctor, Dr. Roberto Paladino; a masseuse named Nick Acosta; his attorney, Roberto Holvino; sparring partner Raul Gorosito; Tito Lectoure; his brother Juan; and his wife Dora and their kids.

For his part, Ali didn't seem to view fighting Bonavena as anything more than a necessary step toward getting in the ring with Frazier. Dave Anderson, a *New York Times* writer, suggested Oscar would actually present a stylistic challenge for Ali, who sometimes needed to feel threatened to excel. The "black kangaroo" comment riled Ali, and getting his blood up was standard operating procedure for selling tickets.

The prefight medical inspection about one week before the December 7 bout is what really knocked Ali off balance. As both men sat on a rubbing table after their inspections, the games began.

"Why you no fight?" Bonavena asked pointedly. "Why you no go [to Vietnam]? You chicken. Chicken. Pipipipipi. Chicken!"

Ali took the antics in stride, appearing thrown by the language barrier. He'd actually emphasized a sort of respect for Argentina and its people several times in the lead-up to the fight, and even when Bonavena got personal, Ali made it known that he didn't think Bonavena was a good representative of his country.

"The Greatest" rattled off a few of his usual lines about how viewers had to watch this fight, how upset Bonavena got him, and so on. Bonavena then leaned in close to Ali and made a pained face before covering his nose with his robe. "Me white, you black," Oscar said. "You stink!" The pressure in the room dropped.

"I'm gonna talk to ya as I whup ya!" Ali yelled. "You never should've started talking! Not with Muhammad Ali!"

"Clye," Oscar quickly replied. "Clye. You Clye? Clye."

Ali corrected him, making it clear he'd taken the bait and been annoyed. At one point Bonavena leaned in and caressed Ali's face. "You need deodorant," he said. "But you lovely. You *maricón*."

Many reporters in attendance would have recognized that word. It led to a death in the ring once.

Madison Square Garden had its share of fatal bouts, though for as many fights that were held at the venue between the 1920s and '30s, it's a miracle so few fighters died. Charles "Bud" Taylor gave the venue its first death in 1924 when Frankie Jerome collapsed after being stopped in the twelfth round and never fully regained consciousness. In 1933, heavyweight Ernie Schaaf died from injuries sustained in his fight with Primo Carnera. And in 1951, Yonkers middleweight Roger Donoghue halted George Flores in eight rounds, with Flores dying a few days later.

But the most-publicized ring death at the Garden happened the last time the homosexual epithet *maricón* had been used so flagrantly. During the weigh-in for a 1961 rematch between welterweight champion Emile Griffith, a bisexual man, and challenger Benny "Kid" Paret, the latter made obscene gestures and called Griffith gay. Paret won a split decision and the welterweight championship, and then, before the third fight 1962, he insulted Griffith again.

Most forget that Paret took a horrible beating from middleweight champion Gene Fullmer and got knocked out in ten rounds between the second and third fights with Griffith. Whether he ever recovered fully from that loss can never be known because, against Griffith in his final bout, Paret got savaged. In the twelfth round, Griffith hurt Paret, who fell into the corner, helpless. Paret became tangled in the ropes and Griffith punched until the champion fell limp and unresponsive, never regaining consciousness. As history remembers it, Paret died for insulting Griffith.

Bonavena's insult had to be translated for Ali, but when Ali heard it he became incensed. The former champion stood up and began shadowboxing, throwing jabs that ended just an inch or two from Bonavena's face.

Bonavena squared up to him, appearing to suggest that they go outside and settle matters in the street. Ali smacked his hand away.

Again the mood quickly changed. Bonavena froze and turned bright red before feinting a punch at Ali, who flinched backward. Bonavena and the Argentine newspaper reporters at the gathering bellowed with laughter, gladly accepting the minor victory as if this was a kind of in-joke. Bonavena turned to his fellow Argentinians and spoke with a fiercely pulsing neck vein.

The scene actually silenced Ali, who looked shaken by Bonavena's unpredictability. "After I whup him," a serious Ali said while lying on his bed a few days later, "I'm gonna civilize that animal."

Finally the NYSAC got involved, threatening to fine both fighters if they didn't knock off the mean-spirited trash talk. It worked. Money talks, of course, and both men shut up.

Bonavena moved his head from side to side according to Gil Clancy's plan at the start of the fight. Just seconds in, however, Bonavena drew a warning for a borderline low punch before finding success with a wild, awkward left hook. Then right as the round ended, Bonavena landed a punch so low it landed on Ali's inner thigh. Bonavena lost the round for it.

Both Howard Cosell and Yank Durham commented from ringside that Ali looked worse post-exile as he struggled with Bonavena's rhythm and style. Indeed, Ali did fight flat-footed, but it also allowed him to sit down on a snapping right hand early in round two.

Drew "Bundini" Brown, Ali's cornerman and friend, kept shouting for Ali to "stick 'em," or to jab and keep his distance. Ali followed instructions but stayed in the center of the ring, leaving him in range of Bonavena's grabbing.

What Clancy said about Ali's inability to fight in the clinch was true, and he wasn't going to magically learn how to do so mid-fight.

Bonavena's mauling broke through, but he paid for it with one-twos and lead right hands to the cheek. More important, Ali simply covered up and fought Bonavena's fight, and the Argentine still couldn't capitalize. Clancy did what he could to convince referee Mark Conn that Ali was pushing Bonavena's head around, which he was, but this was a fight. Bonavena was guilty of some underhanded stuff too.

Ironically, Oscar's light skin became a clear disadvantage in the middle rounds as his cheeks reddened from all the right hands. Still, Cosell and Durham felt Ali looked terrible.

Ali got on his toes more in the sixth and seventh rounds, indicating he didn't really like tussling with Bonavena on the inside. Bonavena responded by landing a few sweeping left hooks and clubbing Ali in the ribs. Clancy's plan—to have Bonavena punch at the same time as Ali—worked, even if only to prevent Ali from throwing in combination.

As round eight began, Ali looked tired and his hands had slowed visibly. He clearly remained the sharper and faster of the two, but Bonavena made a fight of it. And in round nine, the round in which Ali predicted he'd put Bonavena away, both men hurt each other visibly and walked to their respective corners ruffled.

It wasn't clear how fighting inside should have been scored, and much of the wrestling involved illegal tactics like rabbit punching and low blows from Bonavena. Most of the legal punches didn't land cleanly. Still, Ali did little when the fight got inside, and as both men tired, the fight went there more and more.

From a longer range, however, Ali did well with his jab, his right hand, and an occasional counter left hook from rounds eleven through fourteen. The crowd grew restless as Ali gained control of the fight and Bonavena's rushes became less effective, booing loudly before the final round. Although comfortably ahead on the scorecards, Ali was sure to receive criticism for his failure to dominate such a crude opponent.

Bonavena lunged desperately for the first minute of the final round—a last-ditch attempt at upsetting the 6-1 odds against him. Had Bonavena been able to last, he may have fabricated some story about deserving the decision, as he did in both Frazier fights. But Bonavena was never destined to go quietly. Just past the halfway point of round fifteen, Ali landed a fast left hook that took Bonavena's legs out from under him and sent him to the canvas. The three knockdown rule was in effect.

Bonavena's legs were all but gone and it didn't take much to put him down again when he rose. Ali stood over him with his arms over his head, as he had against Zora Folley in 1967. When Bonavena got up unsteadily again, Mark Conn tried to create space and push Ali back. Ali swatted the meek referee's hand away dismissively, smelling blood and craving a knockout.

Four more punches sent Bonavena to his hands and knees for a final time, and there stood Ali, hands raised once more, refusing to give an inch. He wouldn't move. He refused.

But Bonavena got his licks in. "[Bonavena's] my roughest fight to date," Ali told Cosell in the ring right after the fight. It was probably a bit of a verbal slip, given Bonavena's style, but still true. In the eyes of many, Ali appeared very mortal that evening.

Bonavena moped for a few minutes, pacing the ring, likely contemplating what he'd just lost. Then he began hollering in the background as Ali wrapped up his television interview, ranting that Ali was sure to beat Frazier. Then he walked over and apologized for calling Ali a chicken. He never apologized for the other stuff, however.

Both fighters dismissed prefight issues as promotion and free publicity; Ali said he felt no bitterness, and Bonavena said, "In my country, [using the term 'black'] means nothing." For the most part Ali spoke of the upcoming megafight with Frazier, moving the conversation along.

Bonavena put forth a valiant effort, even if it was sloppy, and ended up knocked out for the first time. Ali towered over him and then forgot all about him. If there was a positive aspect in the whole situation, it was that Bonavena had finally become bigger news than the Beatles for one day. Just not the way he wanted.

○ ○ ○

After Luis Ángel Firpo lost spectacularly to Jack Dempsey in 1923, he returned to a sea of Argentine admirers. Rather than accept a whopping $200,000 for an American motion picture contract, he took half of that for a film contract back home. Firpo wanted to bring glory to his country.

Henry L. Farrell, United Press sports correspondent in New York, spent time with Firpo, noting, "Firpo is extremely polite, courteous when approached and painstaking as a host."

When Bonavena arrived home to Ezeiza International Airport after losing to Ali, perhaps a few hundred people showed up. Bonavena was quiet and somber. His lip quivered as he promised he would have gotten up every time even if knocked down a thousand times. He wasn't boisterous or jovial.

Countless fighters have used a well-publicized loss as motivation to do better. Bonavena even did it before with Folley and Frazier. He couldn't do it this time despite being promised more fights at the Garden. A fight against Floyd Patterson six weeks after the Ali bout wound up canceled when Bonavena reported he was "exhausted." In hindsight he may have been exhibiting signs of a concussion given to him by Ali.

Mishaps, injuries, and lame excuses kept Bonavena sidelined for almost all of 1971, the same year 10 percent of the planet tuned in to watch Frazier drill Ali with a left hook in the fifteenth round, sealing his victory and claiming heavyweight supremacy. It's impossible to know how many of Bonavena's injuries and maladies were real since most reports were filtered in part through his personal physician.

Before fighting Ali, Bonavena fought professionally for just under seven years, stepping into the ring fifty-three times. In the next five years before his death, he fought only fourteen times. The only truly meaningful fights during that span were against Floyd Patterson and Ron Lyle. Both fights took months to arrange because of Bonavena's demands and claims of injuries.

Bonavena and Patterson fought more than one year after they had been initially matched. First Bonavena didn't feel right, then he kept aggravating his hand injury, then he suffered a wrist injury in a car accident. Promoters who'd worked with Bonavena previously wanted no part anymore. For years, when Tito Lectoure spoke of Bonavena, it was always following a deep sigh. The promotion for the Patterson bout demonstrated Bonavena's inability to reconcile his notoriety in Argentina with his lack of success in America.

When Gil Clancy brought Emile Griffith to Buenos Aires to challenge middleweight champion Carlos Monzon a few months before Patterson–Bonavena, Ringo hosted them. He ferried Clancy and Griffith around town in his expensive Mercedes, which he could park wherever he wanted. (In New York, Bonavena rented a car and decided he could park it where he pleased too. Days later he called the Garden and said, "Hey, police tow away my car.")

Harry Markson told reporters at a press luncheon for the Patterson–Bonavena bout that Bonavena was "an exasperating man" during negotiations. "I asked [Bonavena] how we could possibly pay him more than Patterson, a two-time champion, and he grunted, 'Yeah, Yeah.'"

Bonavena nearly got what he asked for, earning $70,000, or slightly less than the former champion, plus a percentage of the gate. Bonavena also bragged to reporters about looking at an apartment on New York's East Side. "I go see it yesterday and I like," Bonavena told them. "I think I buy. I want to live here. . . . Then I go back to Buenos Aires. That's my home and that's where I die."

Markson arranged for Bonavena to promote the fight out in front of the Garden on 8th Avenue alongside a bull named Bingo and it apparently helped. Nearly 18,000 fans jammed the Garden to cheer on Patterson, who hit the deck, true to form. Though this time the former champion rose and badly hurt Bonavena two rounds later.

Few newspaper reporters agreed with the unanimous decision for Patterson, but it was like years of mischief boomeranging right back at Bonavena, who broke his left hand for at least the third time in the same spot. Markson was relieved to get past the fight without incident and probably relished seeing Bonavena knocked down a peg another time.

Unfortunately, it also became harder for promoters to gamble the attention Bonavena brought to a fight card against his erratic behavior and outrageous demands. That's at least in part why he only fought far away from where anyone really knew him. After that Patterson bout, however, something else far more sinister kept him away from the bigger fights.

o o o

Bonavena botched a proposed showdown with George Foreman, inconveniencing Boston promoter Sam Silverman in the process.

With the Foreman fight all but signed and done for October of 1972, Bonavena's brother-in-law Roberto alleged the fighter attacked his wife Dora and subsequently punched Roberto on the street in Buenos Aires a month before the scheduled date. Bonavena later called it a "family discussion," and Dora denied anything happened. But something happened substantial enough for Silverman to tell reporters Bonavena's marriage problems killed the Foreman bout, and the couple quickly separated.

Bonavena then hooked up with promoter and manager Loren Cassina, a Canadian fight promoter with television and broadcasting experience, including involvement in arranging the WBA's heavyweight tournament. Right on cue, six months later, Bonavena attacked a tourist and broke his jaw in two places in Mar de Plata, a coastal resort town. Witnesses told police Bonavena fled the scene, and gossip hit the Argentine tabloids quickly, saying he was old and not really a fighter anymore, just a celebrity.

Boxing, never short on predators or prey or predators who become prey, still had plenty to offer someone like Ringo. In New Jersey, Bonavena hooked up with trainer Jimmy De Piano and adviser Sid Peskin, a former fighter whose primary claim to fame was holding the New Jersey record for quickest knockout in a professional bout.

Bonavena then passed on an opportunity to face Jerry Quarry at the Garden when Earnie Shavers pulled out in 1973, claiming he needed more time to prepare. The cancellation marked only the second time in a decade that there was no big July fight card at the famed venue. The truth was that Bonavena's legal issues and failure to pay taxes affected his visa in Argentina and authorities wouldn't let him travel in time to make the fight. He faced four journeymen on a weak U.S. tour instead.

Ron Lyle's handler Bill Daniels set up a Bonavena fight for Denver in 1974. Whether Bonavena knew it or not, this was his final big chance. Before Bonavena could leave Argentina this time, however, police apprehended him and threw him in jail for aggravated assault on that tourist. Bonavena claimed he simply pushed Norberto Bombicino, an architect, but witnesses told police the fighter harassed a young lady and Bombicino tried to defend her. So Bonavena walloped the man, injuring him badly enough to put him out of work for several months. Bombicino sued for $15,000 and Bonavena was let loose.

Lyle, two years older than Bonavena, had limited time to make an attempt at the heavyweight throne. He hired Chickie Ferrara, a New York–area cutman and trainer who had worked Bonavena's corner years earlier.

An undisclosed "liver ailment" sidelined Bonavena and postponed the fight, and the fight again almost derailed at the last moment when Oklahoma promoter Pat O'Grady claimed to have Bonavena under contract. He unsuccessfully petitioned the Colorado State Athletic Commission to have Bonavena suspended. It was Bonavena's typical madness.

After far too many snafus, the fight went forward and the fighters delivered a spirited but sloppy battle to a record Denver crowd. Lyle walked away with a hard-fought decision victory and around $7,000 as Bonavena took a puffy eye and nearly $30,000 with him.

Ken Norton, the heavyweight division's uncrowned champion who broke Ali's jaw and handed "The Greatest" his second defeat, appeared likely to face Bonavena in 1974 and again the following year before injuries and wasted time ensured it couldn't happen.

Apart from Patterson and Lyle, the fourteen opponents Bonavena faced after Ali had a combined record of 210-152-18. These fighters didn't present the challenge Bonavena needed to truly improve in his late twenties and thirties, sixty-something fights into his professional career—all habits, good and bad, had been firmly established. His opposition wasn't going to earn him great praise in the fight community either. That Bonavena remained in *The Ring*'s top-ten heavyweight rankings in 1970–71 and 1973–74 was because of a thinning, top-heavy division.

Whereas Firpo sought to share his glory with fellow Argentines, Bonavena wanted to escape to the United States. After facing Ali, Bonavena only fought twice more at Luna Park, and by then all his talk about leaving Argentina behind echoed far. He fought three times in Italy, the home of his ancestors, "gladiators in Rome," he said.

Juan Perón had once again risen to power in Argentina, but as Bonavena fought in Italy, Perón died. His wife at the time, Isabel, assumed the presidency. The following year, Argentina's military began planning a coup as rebel groups tried to seize a portion of Northwest Argentina. The entire ordeal brought the country, and most travel to and from it, to a standstill.

By the time Oscar defeated Raul Gorosito in his final Luna Park appearance, Jimmy De Piano remained the last holdout keeping Bonavena from utter collapse. The Argentine had become something of a womanizer in addition to his tendency toward chomping cigars and drinking booze.

"[De Piano] say, 'no drink, no smoke, no women.' Fifteen days before fight I no touch girls," Bonavena told *Washington Post* writer Sally Quinn. And he meant *girls*; Bonavena liked very young women, right around eighteen or nineteen years old.

"I don't understand [Aristotle] Onassis," Bonavena said. "He got so much money. Why he got old girl?"

Bonavena scored a points win over Gorosito and stuck around just long enough to field what he said was a legitimate offer from promoter Don King to fight Ali in June of 1976, several months away. As soon as he could, Bonavena left Buenos Aires for the last time. He headed for Las Vegas, where George Foreman's clash with Ron Lyle would take place in January, promoted by King.

The Confortes and Mustang Bridge Ranch were in Nevada too.

Beckoning
Brothels

While prizefights often happened in venues like opera halls and athletic clubs in New York, Boston, and Baltimore, farther out west boxing was left more to develop on its own, surging through big cities and remote towns alike.

In 1902, Nevada prospectors discovered gold about halfway between Reno and Las Vegas. They named it Goldfield, and a town sprang up, increasing to 20,000 residents quickly. In 1906, George "Tex" Rickard teamed with a group of mining investors to raise the funds to stage Joe Gans vs. Battling Nelson for the lightweight title in Goldfield. Gans and Nelson tore at each other for forty-two epic rounds, with Gans winning by disqualification. The fight put Goldfield on the boxing map and kick-started Rickard's legendary promoting career. Less than twenty years later, a fire burned most of Goldfield to the ground.

Las Vegas became a fight hub thanks to the mob and mountains of gambling money that often found its way over from the older and slightly more-tucked-away Reno. But in 1975, the best-known boxing connection in Reno was John "Bud" Traynor. He was involved in most amateur and professional boxing in the area. Traynor also worked as a commissioner with the Nevada State Athletic Commission before he became a promoter.

Traynor had no big fight experience, though—at least compared to a boxing scene like New York or even Buenos Aires. Yet even he had someone looking to use him as a bridge to get in on the action: Conforte.

Conforte was born a few hours from Calabria, Italy, where Bonavena's family came from. He sailed to New York on a ship called the *Rex* in 1937 and his father, a bootlegger, reunited with him in Massachusetts. By the time Conforte was sixteen, he owned a small fruit market in Los Angeles. There he developed an affinity for excursions to Tijuana to gamble and watch bullfights.

"I bought the [fruit market] for practically nothing, because the guy who owned it, he . . . had to go away," Conforte told *Rolling Stone* in 1972. More specifically, the man who previously owned it was sent to an internment camp in 1942 like many other Japanese Americans.

After three separate stints in the U.S. Army, Conforte was discharged in 1950 and quickly started working as a cab driver in Oakland to have an excuse to be out of the service permanently. Conforte tried to run a straight taxi service and wound up constantly driving sailors to and from brothels in Oakland.

"I didn't even know what the word *trick* meant," Conforte said. "I didn't know anything at all about the business. A sailor gets into my cab and says, 'I want to see a girl.' I says, 'What do you mean?' He says, 'Oh, I want to see a girl, I want to have some fun, and I want to pay for it.' And I said, heh, heh, 'Well, I can't help you. I don't know anything about it.' And he got a sad look in his face."

Within days a prostitute got into Conforte's cab and asked him to send any "business" her way. The same sailor from before returned and Conforte made sure to relay what he'd learned. "I says to him, 'Hey, now I know where to take you.' I took him to this girl's apartment, and when he got through, she hands me three dollars."

Conforte became an unofficial john courier in minutes and soon developed into an out-and-out pimp. In 1952, he opened his own Oakland brothel until local authorities shut him down. The following year, he debuted a separate joint in San Francisco, and one month later cops busted down the door with axes and gave Conforte his first arrest and conviction.

Reno, only three hours from Oakland, was the closest gambling hub. Conforte had traveled there a few times for betting and leisure. Naturally, he learned about Nevada's convoluted prostitution laws while visiting. Some people have a knack for spotting opportunities and seizing them, and Conforte was one of those people.

Breaks, Brains & Balls. That was the title of Conforte's autobiography and the three things he said you needed to be successful. But it's almost never that simple.

In 1955, Conforte made his move, opening up the Triangle River Ranch in a portable trailer near Virginia City, about fifteen miles south of Reno. Conforte actually outdid himself with a truly clever operation: The "triangle" referred to the nearby intersection of Lyon, Washoe, and Storey counties. It was like operating in international waters; when authorities or residents said anything about the whoring or tried to shut him down, he'd just tow the trailer to a neighboring county and repeat the process.

A madam named Sally Burgess, one of thirteen daughters born to an Alabama coal miner, opened up her own brothel a few hours away in Fallon around the same time, before eventually getting shut down. She then opened a new brothel in Wadsworth before attracting heat for that one too. Despite more than a decade of experience as a madam, in 1956 Burgess turned to Conforte, a newcomer ten years her junior. Conforte advised her to ignore the law and they parted ways.

The two ran into each other again a month later at a Reno bar called The Doll House as Conforte picked up a girl who needed a ride to his brothel. They soon formed a symbiotic business relationship: Burgess needed protection and Joe needed a madam to manage his business.

Conforte certainly didn't invent the prostitution racket in Reno, and there were several other brothels to compete with, like one owned by Donald Baliotis, the dynamite artist. The competition sometimes led to violence, the kind that draws attention in places where people want peace and quiet.

Local law enforcement found a way around Conforte's savviness when they grew tired of being called out to suspicious brush fires or shots fired near brothels. Conforte could never resist strolling into town with girls on both arms; and when he did, cops would hit him with ambiguous vagrancy charges.

During a trip to Las Vegas in October of 1959, Conforte wound up charged with disorderly conduct and vagrancy alongside an ex-fighter and thief named Jimmy "Kid" Williams, who had his own sordid history.

For starters, Williams, born Mason Grover, had a reputation as a frequent entertainer of prostitutes in Vegas and Reno. While still fighting professionally in 1938, Williams was suspected of being involved with a "white slavery ring." In 1939 he was accused of having violated the Mann Act, and in 1948 he was convicted of killing a Los Angeles cab driver over three dollars. When Williams was arrested with Conforte, he'd just been released from serving a prison sentence for robbing a Vegas club.

Conforte often surrounded himself with characters like Williams, men who'd been sent to jail several times for committing violent, impulsive crimes. The vagrancy charge with Williams also led Conforte to make a huge mistake. The following month, in November of 1959, Conforte tried to extort District Attorney Bill Riggio. Setting up Riggio on a date with an underage girl and threatening to expose everything to the local press took more balls than brains. Riggio caught the threat on tape.

Before Riggio torched Conforte's brothel to celebrate his arrest, authorities found a safe that contained incriminating photos, tax records, and more—all connected to several prominent Nevada figures. That was the leverage Conforte used to stay out of trouble.

Conforte earned a sentence of three to five years in a state penitentiary for extortion in July 1960. He and Sally married, possibly for tax purposes or to salvage financial portions of the business, but the new Mrs. Conforte couldn't handle a brothel on her own.

"I had so much juice," Conforte recalled years later. "I was running a casino inside the prison and had a cook, a maid, and, for three dollars a week, a guy to fan me while I played bridge."

As Joe finished his surprisingly comfortable jail time, a mysterious fire in the middle of the night destroyed three of the trailers he and Sally owned. Upon his release, Joe shifted his approach toward skirting laws and making friends in high places.

The Mustang River Ranch opened in 1964 along the Truckee River, in an area known as the "River District." Joe and Sally bought it and took over completely in 1967, renovated it, and the name changed to Mustang Bridge Ranch. It was a far more permanent location than a towable bungalow and required investment, but it was cleaner and easier to find than the mobile trailers.

Apart from the incident in which old rival Donald Baliotis got caught trying to blow up Mustang Ranch in 1969, Joe did well to quell the violence. It paid off by 1971, when Mustang Ranch became the first fully legal brothel when Storey County passed an ordinance beneficial to Conforte, fulfilling his yearslong dream. His career in sex work was making him famous.

Conforte didn't let this one go. All other brothels got either shut down or were rendered impotent by his increasingly confident band of goons and local authorities who treated him favorably compared to other pimps. He controlled the trade to Reno and back.

But it was more than enforcing a price for sex. Conforte could run red lights without a second thought. When he needed something done, even just getting a custom license plate for his new car, he walked right into the county courthouse for a sit-down with the judge. He schmoozed his way through dinners at the Nevada governor's mansion. Everything, even taxes, were paid in cash.

"Anytime you have a law you can change it," Conforte said. "It's politics. Just politics. Those who are making money illegally in the hotels and from the street in Las Vegas, they have juice in the legislature to do that. Now we got juice in the legislature. I'm not saying that I bribe officials, or anything like that. I don't bribe officials. But it doesn't hurt to be on good terms with them, to be on the right side of them. So you make sure the right people get in office."

Rolling Stone published a feature on Conforte in 1972 titled "Joe Conforte, Crusading Pimp." In it Conforte professed to be liberating women, empowering them by taking them off the streets and making the world's oldest profession safer. He wanted prostitution to be legal everywhere, and he wanted people to know it was Joe Conforte who made it happen.

The lust for *Rolling Stone* journalism around the country peaked in 1971 with Hunter S. Thompson's "Fear and Loathing in Las Vegas" manifesto. In the wake of the tumultuous late 1960s, people devoured it. Writer Robin Green took care to focus not just on Conforte, the pimp, but also to interview the women working at Mustang. There were dozens of them who worked fourteen-hour shifts three weeks in a row, and they could only leave the Mustang compound with an armed escort. There were Asian women and black women, tall and short, veterans and young girls. Everything inside the chain of interconnected trailers was wired with microphones.

Some rooms were themed, but almost all of them had cabinets full of sex toys and kinky outfits. Nothing was off-limits. There were whips, custom lingerie, belts, and nylons. Not to wear but to tightly wrap around the scrotums of customers into that stuff.

"There's some guys, you can slug 'em in the balls as hard as you can and they won't move a muscle," said Kathy, an experienced call girl. "We get some can't come unless you call them a motherfucker."

The women had names like Tiger, Cherry, Yoko, and Gypsy. There was even a side room tucked away for sexual desires that were deemed edgy—usually things like lesbian fantasies and cross-dressing.

Conforte took one of the women, a black prostitute named Chi Chi, into his private office and had her strip and pose for the *Rolling Stone* writer. "Oooh, black meat!" Conforte said with glee. Then he playfully bit Chi Chi's ass, leaving her to clean off his drool.

A business owner couldn't buy the kind of fame the *Rolling Stone* article gave Mustang Ranch. Business took off, and Conforte pretended to be a liberator and justice seeker while robbing these women blind. At Conforte's 1963 tax trial, a girl named Helen Reynolds choked back tears while testifying that 50 percent of her "earnings" were taken from her by Conforte, minus another 10 percent for rent and laundry. Conforte was the definition of a lowlife pimp but worse, because he usually wasn't the only one the women had.

In the 2001 book *Brothel: Mustang Ranch and Its Women*, Dr. Alexa Albert confirmed with several former workers at Mustang that Conforte sometimes required new workers to have outside pimps in addition to his "counsel." Conforte used the other pimps to discipline the women so he could keep his hands clean, and the pimps had the women stay at Mustang where it was safer than being on the streets. That way the pimps could also focus on recruiting new women.

It was all a big scam.

○ ○ ○

Another huge fire at Mustang Ranch in November of 1975 incinerated the trailer complex. It happened the same night law enforcement received calls about someone shooting at passing cars from Mustang Bridge.

Conforte's reaction to this fire, however, proved just how much juice he'd acquired around Reno. Las Vegas authorities quickly located Dan Baliotis, Conforte's old business rival who years earlier tried to blow up Mustang with a stick of dynamite, and held him on suspicion of arson. Baliotis had an unassailable alibi but got slapped with a steep $400,000 bond by District Attorney Virgil Bucchianeri, who Conforte knew well. Despite his alibi, Baliotis remained under suspicion, along with a few others.

It may not have been immediately obvious to Conforte or his wife, but Mustang Ranch teetered on the edge of ruin. Years of ignoring laws, keeping shady records, and running an operation maintained by thugs motivated the residents of Reno and surrounding communities to band together at city council meetings and consider neutralizing Conforte. Several land purchases Conforte made around Reno also complicated his other business relationships. Mustang was operating on borrowed time.

Bonavena's true motive for heading into Nevada is unknown, but, in early 1976, George Foreman and Ron Lyle shook the pillars of heaven with five rounds of epic heavyweight violence at Caesars Palace in Las Vegas. Bonavena attended and heckled both fighters at the post-fight press conference, calling them amateurs.

Since Ali–Bonavena, Ali had twice avenged his loss to Frazier and recaptured the heavyweight title with an unforgettable knockout of Foreman. Don King publicly disputed Bonavena's claim of having received an offer to fight Ali in the summer of 1976, but Bonavena's actions strongly suggested he at least *believed* the offer was authentic.

Bonavena headed deeper into the desert after enlisting the help of Loren Cassina, the old broadcaster, to get another crack at Ali. He was looking for tune-up fights, he said. But too many promoters and managers around the country knew the trouble typically involved when dealing with him. Bonavena still had a name, but along with that came a reputation.

When Bonavena hit Reno, everyone knew it. He drew attention wherever he went. He would walk behind the counter in diners before reaching directly into display cases to grab a pie. Residents didn't know how to react.

In early February, Bonavena attended an amateur fight card at the University of Nevada, Reno, ensuring the card's newspaper coverage saw print. The larger-than-life Bonavena had seen and experienced more of the outside world than nearly anyone in town, and a little mafioso wannabe like Conforte probably revered that.

Cassina lined up an appearance for Bonavena on a fight card promoted by Bud Traynor in late February with plans to leave for Albuquerque the following day. In Albuquerque, Bonavena would fight Roy Rodriguez followed by Earnie Shavers, the world-ranked, murderous-punching heavyweight. Bonavena grew a beard and picked up more English. The *Reno Gazette* sent staff photographer Jim Beazley over to the YMCA where Bonavena trained, and he mugged for the camera and suggested Isabel Perón go back to the kitchen rather than try to lead his home country.

Then he repeatedly referred to George Foreman as "a big monkey" with no provocation. But ignorant remarks from Bonavena weren't novel by this point, and he'd been calling Foreman a monkey and a gorilla to the press for years, since before he upended their scheduled 1972 fight by allegedly committing domestic violence.

No amount of backroom connections or machinations could motivate Bonavena once Reno got into his blood, as Cassina soon discovered. Cassina brought Bonavena to Traynor, who hired Conforte as a matchmaker. After some wrangling, Traynor and Cassina found an opponent for Oscar in Billy Joiner, a Cincinnati heavyweight who was old, weathered, and hadn't won since the 1960s.

The day before the fight, the *Reno Gazette* reported Bonavena applied for a marriage license along with one of Mustang's working girls, Cheryl Ann Rebideaux. Nobody seemed to know about it. When asked by Cassina about it, Bonavena laughed cryptically and denied it.

Another news item in the days leading to the Joiner fight should have concerned Traynor: Conforte applied for and was granted a promoter's license by the state of Nevada. "Now I can do things by myself," Joe said. "I don't have to use other promoters' licenses."

He also didn't have to use Traynor as a middleman anymore. It was Conforte's way of officially breaking into boxing, long known as the sports world's biggest money-laundering operation.

Conforte made advertisement posters for Bonavena–Joiner featuring Bonavena and Sally together. "The Beauty and The Beast," they read. They credited Sally with bringing Bonavena to town.

Bonavena's time in Reno was meant to be spent training, but when he weighed in for the Joiner fight, he'd gained a few pounds since arriving. Then Joiner caused far more trouble than expected. Bonavena scored two knockdowns but punched himself out by the final bell and looked awful. He blamed a lack of quality sparring—a legitimate gripe—but he'd slowed considerably since his younger days and had fallen in love with Reno.

The day after defeating Joiner by unanimous decision, Bonavena refused to sign a new contract and leave with Cassina for Albuquerque. Conforte bought Bonavena's contract and signed Sally on as his new manager. "There are different people here than anywhere in the country," Bonavena told a local reporter. "It's not like Los Angeles. I have more friends here. Maybe I buy a house."

Bonavena purchased a trailer two miles from Mustang Ranch, and Sally agreed to help him gain citizenship and residency. Joe and Sally were in the process of building a brand-new iteration of Mustang Ranch, one with more than fifty trick rooms in a hub-and-spoke style emanating out from a central lobby. There were red carpets, checkered furniture, round beds, Formica counters, and faux-wood paneling.

Conforte, who called himself a devout Catholic, had a collection of crucifixes displayed on the walls of his office. It was unironically kitschy. Back in Buenos Aires, Bonavena used to hang vintage swords on his living room wall.

○ ○ ○

No serious boxing news came out of Reno from the time Bonavena defeated Joiner until his death. Outside newspapers published blurbs about Bonavena possibly facing Ken Norton and even professional wrestler Andre the Giant in a mixed-rules bout, but nothing materialized.

In Reno there was no Charley Goldman, no Gil Glancy, or even a Rago brother to keep Bonavena out of trouble. He drank and smoked Conforte's cigars, borrowed money to head into town for gambling trips, and often stayed overnight at Mustang rather than his trailer.

When Bonavena was home in Buenos Aires, his every move was tabloid fodder. He couldn't go to a nightclub and hang out with younger girls without it making the news, and his legal troubles proved he wasn't nearly as untouchable as he desired to be. In Reno, with Conforte, he could get away with a lot more.

A series of seemingly unrelated events, beginning in early March 1976, set an ultimately deadly chain of events into motion. Mustang Ranch's most recent fire was still being investigated and Conforte wanted answers. He had previously arranged through District Attorney Bucchianeri for anyone with involvement to be granted immunity for a confession. "Whoever did this picked a night when my regular guard was off duty," Conforte said. "This guy knew what he was doing."

Baliotis was released when it was reported he'd been working as an undercover investigator for the state of Nevada in Las Vegas when the fire happened. It was also reported that Baliotis was only arrested after being implicated by a resident of one of Conforte's apartment complexes. But Conforte still wanted polygraphs given to all sorts of people with peripheral involvement in Mustang Ranch, including the landowners, James and Joseph Peri.

In March, the Peris served Conforte with an eviction notice as he left for a trip to Sicily. On returning, Conforte refused to submit to a lie-detector test, and the investigation came to a halt.

Weeks after the eviction notice, Washoe County released a grand jury report that linked Conforte to organized crime members on the East Coast and accused him of bribing officials, at both the local and state levels. Reno newspapers printed scathing takedowns of Conforte almost every day, including raising the possibility that he set the brothel fire himself to collect insurance money.

At least with an indictment, Conforte and others implicated in the grand jury report could defend themselves in court. But grand jury reports don't always lead to indictments, whereas information in them could be floated to the press and do its own damage.

Al Singer and Marvin Goldberg both learned how expensive it was to keep Bonavena entertained. They took their financial hits because they foolishly believed in Bonavena. Now it was Conforte's turn. Plus there was more than one heavyweight for Conforte to look after: Colombian

Bernardo Mercado had signed a management deal with Sally at around the same time as Bonavena and also fought on the Joiner card. Mustang Ranch had become too crowded, too decadent to last as it had. It's easy to believe Bonavena crumbled with it.

Around May 15, Conforte threw a bash to celebrate the opening of the new Mustang Ranch. He shipped in $20,000 in champagne and snacks for more than 4,000 guests. When Conforte uncharacteristically ducked out of his own party, he left behind Sally, Bonavena, and ten to twelve armed Mustang Ranch security guards. Among them were Willard Ross Brymer and John Coletti. Brymer reportedly met Conforte while doing time in a local jail, and Coletti was an old friend and former Bay Area private investigator who became Conforte's bodyguard after the 1975 fire.

Goons with Mustang Ranch badges weaved through the crowd as people toured the Mustang complex. There were rooms with bearskin carpets and rugs with "J. C."—what Conforte liked to be called—embroidered on them. There was a snack kitchen and a lounge for the prostitutes to hang out in. The crown jewel of the complex, Conforte's favorite place, was the "Blue Room," a lavish suite with thick, soft carpet, imported bedding, and thousands of dollars of furniture.

As guests toured Mustang Ranch and soaked up the free booze and hors d'oeuvres, Bonavena, a Beau Brummell, walked around puffing one of Conforte's cigars. "How you like my new joint?" Bonavena asked everyone.

○ ○ ○

Willard Ross Brymer, or Ross as most knew him, had a long criminal history in the Reno area. So did his family. At only eighteen, Brymer robbed an icehouse and got sentenced to a year of probation. Shortly after that, in early 1964, Washoe County sheriff's deputies arrested Brymer for a drunken public disturbance and a judge revoked his probation and sent him to Washoe County jail.

Brymer's little brother Dean couldn't stay out of trouble either. In the span of about two weeks, Dean and Ross led police on separate chases through local streets, both demonstrating that none of the Brymer brothers could be mistaken for criminal masterminds.

At four in the morning on a Saturday, Dean and a man named James Fouchet robbed a restaurant at gunpoint. Police noticed their getaway car parked about a block from the restaurant. It had no license plates and crowbars, gloves, hammers, and a knife laid out on the seats. Officers had time to station themselves down the street to watch for the crooks through binoculars and call in a K-9 unit before Dean and his accomplice exited the restaurant and took off in the car. They were cornered in an alley not far away and hid, but the police dog saw their feet hanging off a roof. Dean didn't want to come down, "but when I pointed my hand cannon at them they changed their minds," the arresting officer said.

Ross found a way to outdo his younger brother when he and a friend robbed slot machines in a bar. The coins and copper mugs the men used weighed nearly 150 pounds and slowed the men enough for police to catch up and chase them in cruisers. Ross and his partner crashed over someone's fence and drove through their yard and flower garden, hitting a telephone pole a block away before getting captured and booked on robbery charges. Ross had been bailed out of jail on drug charges only eight hours earlier.

At twenty, Dean got sentenced to two years in prison for a previous drug conviction and his role in the restaurant robbery and subsequent chase.

In 1968, following arrests for minor marijuana charges, a judge sentenced Ross Brymer to four years of jail time for the burglary of Carl & Martin's Bar in Reno. Then in 1972, after being released, he got arrested again along with his wife Linda for marijuana possession and was later charged with attempting to bribe a witness in one of his cases. Both Brymer and his wife went to trial. Linda was found not guilty; Brymer was sentenced to another four years. While Brymer served time, Linda was granted a divorce.

It's not clear when Ross began working for Conforte at Mustang Ranch, but he made his presence felt when he was there. "Brymer was six-foot-three, 230 pounds, a fistfighter, an ass-kicker, a crowd-control man," wrote Barry Farrell for *New York* magazine. "He would stand by cracking his knuckles in embarrassment when Conforte introduced him [by saying], 'This guy, I ain't lying, can take two heads and mash 'em together like cantaloupes.'"

According to Farrell, Brymer had plans to leave the business and go straight, to purchase a saloon down south in Mina before he killed Bonavena. That wouldn't explain why the application to buy the joint was filed by Brymer's brother John, or why in late April 1976, a month before shooting Bonavena, Brymer decided to hop down from one of the Mustang Ranch guard towers and assault three auto-wrecking-yard employees having lunch in their car nearby.

The *Nevada State Journal* reported Brymer charged the car the men sat in, fired two shots into the air with his rifle, and ordered the men out at gunpoint before kicking them in the head. Brymer then told everyone to get back into the car and kicked the door as it drove away. The men in the car watched as Brymer returned to the guard tower. He didn't seem like a man trying to escape the fast life.

Conforte told conflicting stories about Brymer's hostility toward Bonavena, whose trailer was parked near Brymer's. Once he said Brymer feuded with the fighter about one of Mustang's women, and another time he said Bonavena's behavior at the grand opening sent Brymer into a frenzy.

Conforte, apparently incensed by Bonavena daring to move in on his turf—and convinced that Sally was in on it—banished Sally and Bonavena from the Mustang property two days after the grand opening, ordering security to stop them if they tried to come back. The following day, Bonavena came back from a workout to find his trailer ransacked and his possessions, including his passport and beloved wardrobe, incinerated. Bonavena and Sally hopped in the new Mercury Cougar she bought him and drove to the Storey County sheriff's headquarters in Virginia City. There they filed a complaint about the fire and mentioned threats that accompanied their expulsion from Mustang Ranch.

From Virginia City they drove to San Francisco to replace Bonavena's burned passport, Sally later told investigators. But while there they stopped at the Argentine Embassy and left a message for Consul Adolpho Nanclares. "Anything from here on that may happen to me, be it accident or assassination attempt can be attributed to the responsibility of Mr. Conforte," Bonavena wrote.

After Bonavena's death, Sally told police they received a phone call while in San Francisco, warning them not to return to Reno. She said she wanted a police escort home. Upon returning to Reno, Bonavena cried wolf.

Dora Raffa, Bonavena's estranged wife, maintained for decades that Bonavena called her from Reno after the San Francisco trip saying his life had been threatened. He said he only wanted to fight and fell for a scam. She wasn't even sure whether to take the phone call seriously. Dora never spoke to him again after that.

Conforte told investigators he had one final conversation with Bonavena sometime between May 16 and May 21. Conforte said he dissolved Bonavena's contract, told him to board the first flight back to Buenos Aires, and gave him a fistful of hundred-dollar bills and a check for $7,500.

A card dealer at the Sundowner casino told investigators Bonavena stayed there several hours, drinking and gambling. At around 4:30 a.m., she said, Bonavena took a phone call and left in a hurry, ending up in the parking lot of Mustang Ranch.

He never left that parking lot.

○ ○ ○

No one alive knows why Bonavena drove from the Sundowner casino over to Mustang Ranch at dawn. Everyone who happened to be at Mustang when Bonavena arrived, apart from the johns, was an employee paid by Conforte. Each had their own allegiance to or relationship with Joe or Sally. Consistent among them, though, was the account of what happened in front of Mustang Ranch around 6 a.m. on May 22, 1976.

According to witnesses present, Bonavena parked his Cougar a few strides from Mustang's front entrance, a locked gate topped with razor wire. He ran to the gate and grabbed the fence, shaking it and ringing the security buzzer.

Sally's niece, Neva Tate, happened to be working the security desk, and she called for Conforte's bodyguard, John Colletti, who went out to calm Bonavena down but forgot his revolver; he'd been given a concealed weapon permit two days earlier. According to Tate, Colletti and Bonavena argued back and forth for several minutes, Bonavena asking, "Why Joe no like me?"

In his autobiography, *Breaks, Brains & Balls*, an incredibly poorly edited, rambling hagiography, Conforte wrote, "Bonavena told [Colletti], 'I fucked Joe's wife, and now I'm going in to kill Joe!'"

As Bonavena haggled with Colletti, Tate rang for Ross Brymer, who first went to the Blue Room to wake Conforte. When Conforte wouldn't respond, Brymer headed toward the security area where they stored three shotguns, but he couldn't find any shells there. Joe Peri Jr., son of one of the Peris who owned the land Mustang sat on, retrieved a .30-06 hunting rifle from the guard tower and Brymer grabbed it and chambered a round.

In Colletti's recorded statement to investigators, he said he told Bonavena, "Oscar, you're not allowed here. You were told to stay away and we have orders to keep you away."

Every account agreed that Bonavena demanded to see Conforte. But according to Colletti, Bonavena turned slowly toward his car, keeping his eyes trained on Conforte's security guard, and then began rummaging through his car, as if to find something. A voice yelled, "Freeze!" and Colletti said Bonavena's head popped up as if the command got his attention, then the crack of a rifle shot echoed through the hills.

"It's the flame," Bonavena said as he tapped his chest, not long after arriving in Reno. "When the flame is OK, the fighter is alright. When it's gone. . . ."

A .30-06 bullet entered Bonavena's chest a few inches left from the midline, directly at heart level. When the bullet pierced Bonavena's heart, the heart literally exploded, as fluid-filled organs tend to do. There was never any chance of surviving that wound.

Colletti looked up over his shoulder after the rifle fired and saw Brymer holding the gun, but later nobody would admit to actually seeing the entire shooting. Brymer calmly walked back into the kitchen area of the brothel and poured himself a bowl of cereal and a glass of orange juice. Someone placed a 911 call, and Washoe County officers and their SWAT team were the first law enforcement to officially arrive. By then Conforte had been jarred awake by phone calls from Mustang's front desk and took control of the murder scene, though Brymer locked himself in one of the rooms.

"So we got a dead man here," remarked Conforte. "So what?"

The scene quickly became frenzied, however, and Conforte began skating restless circles around Bonavena's corpse. He barked and ranted at the authorities, calling them "dogs" until they retreated across county lines about a quarter-mile from the ranch. It took about an hour for Storey County sheriff Bob Del Carlo to arrive and restore a semblance of order.

Brymer exited the compound not long after Del Carlo made his appearance, and the sheriff escorted him to Nevada State Prison in Carson City, where he was held without bail pending formal charges.

The same day as the shooting, the *Reno Evening Gazette* published a crime-scene photo and word quickly spread that Oscar Bonavena had been shot and killed out front of America's most famous brothel. The photographer, Jim Beazley, was the same one who took photos for Bonavena's first news feature in Reno back in February.

Beazley told investigators that Storey County sheriff's deputy Bill Tilton gave him permission to photograph the scene, and he said he arrived to see a brothel employee hosing down part of the sidewalk near Bonavena. Beazley began snapping his camera and heard Conforte order Colletti to chase him down and confiscate a roll of film. Colletti obliged.

Every day a new detail emerged during the investigation. Bonavena had actually married Cheryl Rebideaux and had the marriage annulled. Conforte switched the name on the brothel license application from Sally's to his. The gun used to kill Bonavena belonged to Colletti. Neither of the guns found on Bonavena's corpse belonged to him. And Bonavena's corpse had clearly been moved before authorities got there.

For days Bonavena's killing remained an international news item, ironically how he would have preferred it.

Just days after the crime, however, Conforte, Colletti, and Bernardo Mercado all skipped town together, but in different cars. "Joe, may I ask you now where the hell we are going?" Colletti claimed he said. "Why three cars? I'd like to know where in the hell we're going."

Reno authorities issued a warrant for Colletti's arrest as a material witness to Bonavena's death and tracked the trio down in Martinez, California, where Conforte owned a property, and arrested Colletti.

Constant news updates didn't stop for almost a month. Bonavena's death was easily the most popular ongoing local story.

Meanwhile, back in Argentina, magazines like *El Siete Días*, *Revista Goles*, and *El Gráfico* seized on the details and plastered photos of everyone involved across their article features. It turned quickly into a real-life soap opera. Headlines said in bold, "They want to save Ringo's killer!"

"I want to say that all Argentine writers are the biggest sensationalists and liars in the world," Conforte phoned to a reporter at a local paper after Oscar's death.

In the United States, the case against Brymer turned into a case against Conforte. That turned into a tax-avoidance case against Joe and Sally Conforte, which then became a much wider investigation into Conforte's bribes and corruption around Reno.

Bonavena's death slowly faded to a footnote in America, despite being the catalyst to this saga's crescendo.

o o o

Vicente Bonavena used to look after Oscar when they were kids. Oscar's leg issues required surgical correction at one of the various hospitals that sprung up in place of *la quema*, a trash incinerator necessary to rid a teeming Parque Patricios of its rubbish. Oscar couldn't run well for much of his youth and he walked funny too.

When Bonavena went to Reno, Vicente wasn't there to babysit him. Instead a distraught Vicente had to fly to Reno and pick up his little brother's remains, helping Bonavena make one last retreat home from this barbaric country.

Vicente arrived back in Buenos Aires with Bonavena's body on May 28. All day May 29, Oscar lay in state at Luna Park, where the ring would normally be. According to police, more than 150,000 mourners paid their respects by either nodding at, kissing, or clutching onto Ringo's body, including light heavyweight champion Victor Galíndez and even middleweight champion Carlos Monzon, who Oscar had a slight feud with.

El Cronista published photos of Oscar's mother Dominga weeping as she clutched her dead son's face. *Goles* did them one better, showing a much larger photo of Dora in a white dress sobbing as she got one final look at her estranged husband. *El Gráfico* outdid them all with a several-page spread of photos, funeral coverage, and a few new, unconsidered motives.

It was easy to forget amid the raunchy carnival of dollar-store diversion that a human being lost his life. There would be no more dancing and clowning with Adriana, and Natalio wouldn't know much of his father. Dora called Bonavena her "estranged husband" when contacted by the media, but real tears rolled down her cheeks and onto Bonavena's cold, pale body as she caressed his hair gently. He wore a beautifully fitted suit adorned with crosses, well-dressed even for his own wake.

"Muerto, estoy enterrado dentro de ti," Oscar once wrote in a letter to Dora. "Dead, I am buried inside you," it reads literally. The handwriting was so awful it looked like something only a small child could write, and it was impossible to know if Oscar was being literal, romantically abstract, or silly.

On May 30, a thirty-eight-car funeral procession slowly made its way to *Cementario de la Chacarita,* just south of the Colegiales neighborhood. José María Gatica was buried there in 1963 and Juan Perón in 1974 followed by poet, composer, and amateur boxer Cátulo Castillo in 1975. Pascual Pérez would be buried there in 1977. Bonavena's uncle Antonio Bonavena, the famous composer, rested there too.

○ ○ ○

Details of the moments leading to Bonavena's killing and immediately afterward only became more obscured with time. District Attorney Virgil Bucchianeri reportedly believed that he knew exactly what happened and pressed forward with his case against Brymer. Conforte put his beloved, tacky restaurant Cabin in the Sky, or "Cab 'inna Sky" as he called it, up as collateral and posted Brymer's bond a month after Bonavena's death.

The woman Bonavena married before his death, Cheryl Rebideaux, skipped town to Hawaii with a few girlfriends when issued a bench warrant to testify in the trial. U.S. District Attorney Ray Pike suggested in court that Rebideaux left town, fearing those she could potentially testify against, which she denied.

"One of the girls was afraid to go home because her husband had threatened her," Rebideaux testified. "She got us all revved up on the idea [of going to Hawaii]."

Jerry Polaha, Brymer's attorney, attempted to have the case thrown out by filing a writ of habeas corpus before advising Brymer to plead innocent to murder. Brymer then had to post bail for the incident a few weeks before Bonavena's death in which he assaulted three men with a rifle near Mustang Ranch.

Grand jury hearings dotted the U.S. Attorney's Office schedule in the months after the crime, but the subject of the hearings gradually became how much influence Conforte held in the Nevada counties surrounding Reno.

A man named Julio Morales approached the media almost immediately after Bonavena's death. He was Bonavena's assistant and friend, who'd spent some time with him in Reno, and he complicated the investigation by claiming he'd never left Bonavena's side for even an instant while in

Reno and that Bonavena never married Cheryl Rebideaux. Months later Morales released his own book about Bonavena's death, despite admitting he was already in Buenos Aires when he heard the news. He maintained that Bonavena never got married, even when confronted with the actual marriage license. Morales also told the *Miami Herald* he planned to sell the rights to the book as a screenplay.

Conforte's old foe, Donald Baliotis, retired as an investigator to work on a case he filed against Conforte in Las Vegas. In his suit he alleged Reno-area officials only issued a warrant for his arrest at the behest of Conforte, and did so without probable cause. Baliotis's suit actually led to a far-more-important action against Conforte: On the eve of the one-year anniversary of Bonavena's death, Dora filed a $7 million wrongful death lawsuit on behalf of her children against Brymer and the Confortes in Reno.

In October of 1977, as the case against Brymer continued, it became apparent just how much of Reno's day-to-day operations Conforte influenced. District Court Judge Frank Gregory declared a mistrial when a prospective juror on the case claimed to have seen Conforte consorting with another juror. A separate member interviewed for a jury spot said she spoke with Conforte ahead of the hearing.

That's when Conforte's trailer parks and apartment complexes wound up working against him. Judge Gregory later told the *Reno Gazette* that a husband and wife actually ended up in the same jury panel, in addition to several residents of Conforte's properties. Panel members all knew Conforte or knew of him. The well was poisoned.

Shortly after the mistrial, a group of Argentine journalists ransacked Judge Gregory's office in Carson City and had to be removed by a sheriff. Mario Laura Avignolo of Argentina's version of *People* magazine, called *Gente*, said Sally flew to Buenos Aires and attempted to settle the big lawsuit. Conforte called the *Reno Gazette* to claim the reports were a lie.

That was one of Conforte's many foibles. He couldn't keep his mouth shut. He would occasionally refuse all press phone calls before speaking recklessly to some backwoods newspaper. He told *Gold Hill News*, for example, that Bonavena arrived at Mustang Ranch to assassinate him on the morning he died. That was a full two years before he testified at trial.

Conforte all but stopped heading into town with women on his arm, gnashing on cigars, and he stayed away from Cab 'inna Sky. The people around Reno made it clear in town meetings that they resented the attention Conforte had drawn.

Around the same time, Joe and Sally faced federal tax evasion charges thanks to Joe Peri Jr., who reportedly stole a discarded "trick sheet"—a yellow, lined sheet of paper detailing a day's business at Mustang Ranch—and handed it over to federal investigators. Peri handed Brymer the weapon to kill Bonavena and a year later handed the feds the weapon to kill Conforte.

Conforte knew the routine. The charges weren't going away this time either. More jail time loomed.

Even out on bail, Ross Brymer kept getting into trouble. In November of 1977, federal agents took him into custody, charging him with harboring a fugitive and accessory to bank robbery. A jury found him innocent in early 1978, but he'd been in and out of jail since he was a teenager and had no reason or means to stop.

Brymer's defense evolved from charging that the prosecution couldn't even prove he pulled the trigger on the gun that killed Bonavena to saying that Brymer did pull the trigger but fired a warning shot over Bonavena's head that magically hit him directly in the heart instead. Finally the defense settled on the idea that Brymer moved to aim the gun and it fired by accident, and somehow the bullet found its mark.

One month later, Polaha struck a deal with Bucchianeri and Brymer pleaded no contest to involuntary manslaughter. The deal bypassed a trial, so Judge Gregory held a one-day evidentiary hearing to sort out the details of the case. Conforte dramatically brought up a new assertion that it was actually Bonavena who threatened *him* in the days before his death. He said he conveniently just learned of the threats from Sally days earlier, nearly two years after the killing.

Following a recommendation that Brymer spend ten years behind bars, Judge Gregory handed down a two-year prison sentence. Then the state of Nevada and the feds hammered away at the Confortes. Joe began showing up in town again to mingle and make good, but most of his admirers were long gone. The flaunting had the opposite effect: Authorities just worked harder to bust him.

The same day Brymer walked out of prison in July of 1979, having served just under eighteen months of his two-year sentence, Conforte was arrested and held on charges of bribing Lyon County District Attorney John Giomi. The indictment alleged Conforte met with Giomi and offered him vacations, women, a Ferrari, and more if he helped Conforte procure a brothel license in Lyon County. In the twenty years since Conforte's trial for extortion, the only thing that changed was the level of sophistication of his scams.

Oscar Bonavena probably would have liked how the 1980s were loud, fun, and decadent. But the '80s weren't kind to Joe Conforte from the start. Nevada counties around Reno called grand juries to investigate Conforte and find out which officials he bought. Most of those grand jury hearings wound up a waste of resources, however, even if they validated community concerns.

In April of 1980, a state investigator named Gene Combs, who unsuccessfully ran for Storey County sheriff two years earlier, alleged a direct "pipeline" between the grand jury members and Conforte. He said Storey County District Attorney Jack Christensen should be removed from office for failing to challenge the grand jury picks.

Members of the grand jury panel included Shirley Colletti, the wife of Conforte's bodyguard John Colletti, and James "Slats" Slattery, a former state senator and longtime friend of Conforte. Mounting evidence emphasized that an impartial trial, grand jury, dinner, or even a quick chat over a cigarette were impossible to have around Reno, so long as they pertained to Joe Conforte. He knew too many people, wined and dined too many officials.

Prosecuting Conforte at the local level wouldn't be easy. Washoe County Special Prosecutor Mills Lane was assigned to investigate the connections between county officials. Within weeks, Christensen and Conforte's attorneys filed motions to drastically limit the scope of Lane's investigation.

Lane, an ex-U.S. Marine and ex-professional fighter with more than a decade of experience working the Nevada boxing scene as a judge and referee, had no issue speaking up about the blatant corruption snuffing out an investigation about corruption. "I'm not going to go up and do a half-ass job," Lane told Phil Barber of the *Reno Gazette*. "If they want me [off the investigation], they better get a court order to get me out."

The inter-county squabbling made its way to the Nevada Supreme Court, which struck down Christensen's attempts to remove Lane. Eventually Lane was hamstrung by Conforte pleading the Fifth Amendment before a grand jury.

Undeterred, the IRS issued tax liens against Mustang Ranch and Conforte's other properties, forcing him to consider selling his brothel for the first time.

Giomi's bribery case against Conforte moved forward, and Giomi said he feared for his family's safety because of his involvement. Then, "I put myself with my God and I had no more anxieties," he said.

Conforte exhausted every appeal option during his tax evasion trial and, facing mounting allegations and at least five years in a federal prison, he disappeared in December of 1980. The timing couldn't have been better to add one final layer to Bonavena's killing. The following month, notorious West Coast mob hitman Aladena "Jimmy the Weasel" Frattiano alleged in the book *The Last Mafioso* by Ovid Demaris that, while in San Francisco, Bonavena and Sally Conforte asked to have Joe Conforte killed. Frattiano said Conforte then summoned the mobster to Mustang Ranch with a panicked phone call. There Conforte asked Frattiano to kill Sally, the hitman said.

"How's your nerve?" Conforte asked.

"What are you talkin' about?" Frattiano responded.

"How do you feel about icing a woman? Have you ever iced one before?"

"Joe, don't come up with them questions. Are you a prosecutor?"

"Let's say it's Sally. Now, I'm not saying it is, you understand? I'm just trying to get a ballpark figure. Would $10,000 do?"

"Let's lay it out in the open. If it's Sally, it's going to be one hundred grand. Think it over and let me know and I'll let you know."

Two weeks later, Brymer killed Bonavena.

Much of this story is obscured by time and levels of absurdity. Bonavena *might* have had an affair with Conforte's wife, and he *may* have committed assault on his own wife. But he definitely left in the lurch far too many people who helped him. The question is whether he deserved to be relegated to being just a dead human slumped under a wrinkled white sheet, marked by a black arrow on a newspaper page.

○ ○ ○

Oscar Bonavena will always have Buenos Aires, where he's still a saint and martyr.

Fútbol, its own international religion, infiltrated Argentina even more successfully than boxing, and over time athletic clubs all over Buenos Aires created their own *fútbol* teams, like Parque Patricios' Club Atlético Huracán. Bonavena wore the Huracán jersey with pride. The Club built a life-sized statue of Bonavena that sits in the stands of its stadium, contorting its playful face.

Like most organized *fútbol* clubs, Huracán traditionally chants a signature tune during matches: *"¡Somos del barrio, del barrio de la Quema, somos del barrio de Ringo Bonavena!"*

"We are from the neighborhood, the neighborhood of la Quema, we are from the neighborhood of Ringo Bonavena!"

SELECTED SOURCES

Albany Democrat-Herald, *Anderson Herald*, *Arizona Republic*, *Austin American Statesman*, *Baltimore Sun*, *Boston Herald*, *Boxing & Wrestling*, *Boxing Illustrated*, *Chicago Daily News*, *Hartford Courant*, *High Point Enterprise*, *Jersey Journal*, *The Jewish Transcript*, *Kingston Daily Freeman*, *Las Vegas Review-Journal*, *Las Vegas Sun*, *Los Angeles Times*, *Mason Valley News*, *Miami Herald*, *The Montreal Gazette*, *Nevada State Journal*, *New York Daily News*, *New York* magazine, *The New York Times*, *Newark Star-Ledger*, *The Oregonian*, *The Palladium-Item*, *Philadelphia Daily News*, *Philadelphia Inquirer*, *The Placer Herald*, *Press and Sun Bulletin*, *Redlands Daily Facts*, *Reno Gazette-Journal*, *The Ring*, *Rolling Stone*, *Sacramento Bee*, *San Francisco Examiner*, *Seattle Daily Times*, *Sports Illustrated*, *Van Nuys Valley News*, *Zanesville Times-Recorder*

ARGENTINE SOURCES

El Gráfico, *Goles*, *Ultima Hora*

BOOKS

Bordón, Juan Manuel. *Luna Park: El Estadio Del Pueblo, El Ring Del Poder*. Buenos Aires: Sudamericana, 2017.

Conforte, Joe, with David Toll. *Breaks, Brains & Balls*. Virginia City, Nevada: Gold Hill Publishing Co., 2011.

Ryan, Joe. *Heavyweight Boxing in the 1970s: The Great Fighters and Rivalries*. Jefferson, North Carolina: McFarland and Co., 2013.

Remnick, David. *King of the World: Muhammad Ali and the Rise of an American Hero*. New York: Random House, 1998.

Sullivan, Russell. *Rocky Marciano: The Rock of His Times*. Champaign, Illinois: University of Illinois Press, 2002.

YOUTUBE

Many videos of Oscar Bonavena can be readily found on YouTube, including full versions of his biggest fights. There are also many interviews of Bonavena in Spanish conducted by several Argentine reporters, some of which give better insight into the heavyweight's family life, and all of which feature his unmistakable high-pitched and musical way of speaking.

SPECIAL THANKS

Thanks to those who believed in me and those who had patience.

ABOUT THE AUTHOR

Patrick Connor is originally from San Diego, California. His work has been featured in many publications, including *The Guardian*, *The Oregonian*, and *Boxing News*. He is also a member of the Boxing Writers Association of America and the International Boxing Research Organization. This is his first book. He lives with his family in Vancouver, Washington.

Shot at a Brothel is set in 9.5-point Palatino, which was designed by Hermann Zapf and released initially in 1949 by the Stempel foundry and later by other companies, most notably the Mergenthaler Linotype Company. Named after the sixteenth-century Italian master of calligraphy Giovanni Battista Palatino, Palatino is based on the humanist typefaces of the Italian Renaissance, and reflects Zapf's expertise as a calligrapher. Copyeditor for this project was Shannon LeMay-Finn. The book was designed by Brad Norr Design, Minneapolis, Minnesota, and typeset by New Best-set Typesetters Ltd.

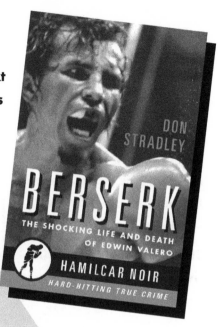

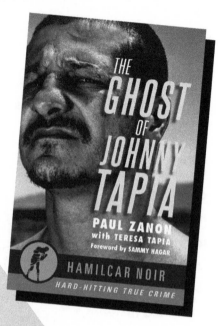

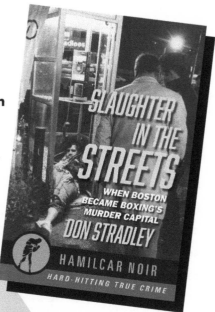

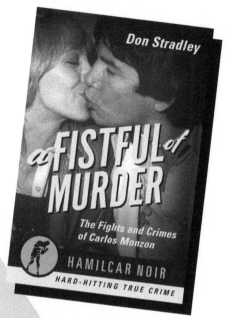

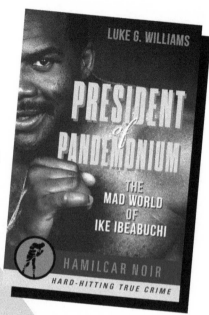

BORN FROM A BOXING MIND

Established in 2003, Rival Boxing Gear has since become a global leader in the industry, with some of the best fighters in the world having entrusted their hands to us. The RFX-Guerrero Pro Fight Glove has been used by some of boxing's greatest champions in World Title fights.